MYTHOLOGY

CW01558988

Greek, Norse and Egyptian Mythology

BY

Stephan Weaver

GREEK MYTHOLOGY

NORSE MYTHOLOGY

EGYPTIAN MYTHOLOGY

GREEK MYTHOLOGY

Greek mythology is indisputably one of the most riveting literary relics and religions of history that continues to fascinate all of humanity. The colorful gods and their enthralling feuds and affairs, the wars, the rivalry—it is an unending stream of allure.

Despite the impalpable aspects of the mythologies of ancient Greeks though, it still serves as the matchless window through which humanity can gaze at what kinds of people roamed the earth even before the birth of Christ. Greek mythology isn't just a batch of incredibly innovative tales patched up together to marvel and entertain the mind, it's what verifies the age-long supremacy of human imagination and cravings for order and answers.

This eBook attempts to look at the Titans, the great Olympians, the Heroes, the Trojan War and quite a few interesting facts about the gods you most certainly would be surprised to learn.

CHAPTER I

Greek Mythology

Ancient Greece and its civilization are part of what constitute the greatest part of world history. And what's incredibly unique is how the Greeks had more power and influence over the world because of their mythologies.

Greek mythology is of great significance, not only did it take the world by its breath but it also managed to outlive the ruling days of Greece and become a dominant component of European culture. As a matter of fact, Greek mythology is still radiant in its influence in many inventive works to this very day.

History of Greek Mythology

Greek mythology emerged from a large assemblage of narratives or story-telling and figurative arts such as Votive gifts and Vase paintings. It was an oral tradition, and for centuries the stories were passed down from one generation to the next by word of mouth. According to the studies of Martin Nilsson (1874 – 1967), a Swedish scholar, the root of the myths go back to the Minoans on the island near Crete and the Mycenaeas on the mainland Greece.

The stories broadly explore the nature of the world, its origin and significance; they give a detailed account of their deities, demigods, heroes and mythical creatures such as the Kentauroi race, which were half man and half horse, their lives and the amusingly brave adventures they embarked upon.

As earlier stated, though Greek mythology was an oral tradition. And so every generation had the liberty to alter, add or omit sections that were (in their judgment) unfavorable or unfitting to the occasion. With the original facts therefore altered, the stories often conflicted. But then came the literature era and Greek mythology began to get its confirmation in writing and finally managed to obtain a solid ground in human history.

The main informants of the mythology of ancient Greeks are the written works of Homer and Hesiod, which date back to 700 B.C. One of the greatest and most fascinating epic poems written in that century was *Iliad* and *Odyssey*, which according to historians were written by the poet Homer.

A legion of poets and dramatists then soon followed in the footsteps of Homer and Hesiod: Aeschylus (525-456 BC), Euripides (485-406 BC), Pindar (518-438 BC), and Sophocles (495-406 BC) are but a few. Tantamount to those who amplified the virtues of Greek Gods, Goddesses, Heroes and all that the Greek mythology encompasses by way of rhythmic poetry, there were also those – historians, philosophers, travelers, and geographers – who penned both their complimentary and disapproving views on these fictitious entities.

'The situation has been entirely reversed since the days when thinkers thought of the stars as without souls. Yet even then they were object of admiration, and the conviction which is now actually held was suspected by those who embarked on exactness: that in no way could the stars as soulless things keep so precisely to marvelous calculations, if they did not possess intelligence. Some even then were bold enough to venture this very proposition and they say that it was reason that had ordained everything in the sky. But these very men were deceived about the nature of the soul, namely that it is older than the bodies; they imagined it as younger and thus so to speak ruined everything, and most of all themselves.'

— Plato

These writings aren't just relics of history; they are history themselves. Some of these pieces have even lead curious historians and archeologists to unraveling great discoveries. For instance, in 1870 Heinrich Schliemann, a German archaeologist resting his faith on the guidance provided by Homer's *Iliad*, went out on an excavation in northwestern Turkey to find the ancient city of Troy. And much to everyone's surprise, it wasn't long before he found the remains of a buried city along with gold, pottery, silver and much besides.

CHAPTER II

The Twelve Titans

A vile yet unchallengeable tribe of deities, the Titans ruled over the universe before the Olympian gods. The Twelve Titans were the offspring of the primordial Uranus (Heaven) and Gaia (Earth). They were enormous deities who possessed incredible power and ruled during the period of the legendary Golden Age. These gods toppled their father Uranus who was the earliest ruler of the universe.

Their act of usurpation was prompted by their mother Gaia who found her husband's actions intolerable. Because of the jealousy Uranus had over his children, he hid them all in the huge body of Gaia till she could no longer endure the strain and implored her kids to retaliate on their horrendous father.

There were six sons, six daughters and twelve Uranides:

Cronus

Cronus was the ruler of the Titans and Eternal Time and. The youngest of the Titans, Cronus was wedded to his sibling Rhea. Although Cronus had declared his desire for toppling Uranus emanated from his father's indecent and extreme rule, Cronus himself adapted his father's vice and cunning traits.

In the battle of Titanomachy, his son Zeus led a successful rebellion against the Titans and toppled him.

Okeanos (Oceanus)

Eldest Titan, Okeanos was the God of fresh water river and rain. The name Okeanosindicates the connection with the mythical stream which encircles the world. He was the husband of Tethys, a nurse who was probably thought to distribute the water to earth. The different river-gods (consisting of the Styx and Nile) and Oceanids were their children.

Iapetus ("the Piercer")

Son of Gaia and Uranus, Iapetus was a Titan god. He was amongst the four siblings who played a role in his father's castration. He married Clymene or Asia (the daughter of Tethys and Okeanos). Epimetheus, Atlas, Menoetius and Prometheus were his children. It's said to be that he wedded Themis (his sibling) and fathered Prometheus. Iapetusis often considered as the Titan god of the mortal life span.

Iapetus' sons were also described to have some of the worst of human traits: Prometheus, on an intellectual level, was excessively cunning; Epimetheus a guileless fool; Atlas overly bold; Menoetius conceited and given to hasty and violent actions. Their natural traits eventuated in their downfall. Iapetus and his family were believed to be the ancestors of humanity.

Hyperion

Hyperion ('Helios Hyperion') is the God of the Sun. He was amongst the sibling conspirators involved in the usurpation of Uranus; the siblings themselves were later removed from power by the Olympians.

Hyperion was married to his sister TitanessTheia or Euryphaessa, which are the parents of Helios, Selene and Eos.

Crius (Kreios or Krios)

Crius married his half-sister Eurybia who was the child of Pontus and Gaia. He was the father of Astraios, Perses and Pallas. He was often believed to be a ram-shaped god.

Coeus (also Koios)

Coeus is the god of intellect, wisdom and query. Wedded to his sister Phoebe, he fathered Asteria and Leto. Leto was married to Zeus. After the defeat of the Titans by the Olympian gods, he along with all the Titans was condemned to Tartarus (a region at the earth's lower region, even further than the underworld) for eternity.

Rhea

Rhea (or Rheia) is a goddess of motherhood, generation and female fertility. She was the sister and wife of Cronus. She was also the mother of the Olympian gods: Zeus, Hera, Hestia, Demeter, Hades and Poseidon. Upon hearing the warning of his mother Gaia about his imminent usurpation by his children, Cronus took the extreme precaution and swallowed his offspring the instant they were born. He managed to ingest all his children but one: Zues. When Rhea was pregnant with him she fooled Cronus into believing a stone wrapped in swaddling clothes was Zeus. He swallowed the stone assuming that it was his youngest son Zeus.

Zeus grew to maturity and commenced to raise a power against his father. He not only succeeded in toppling his father but also managed to have him regurgitate his siblings.

Tethys

Tethys was a Titan goddess who was the daughter of Gaia and Uranus. She was the goddess of the sources of fresh water which nourishes the earth. She was the consort of Oceanus; her children were Okeanides (Springs, Streams, Fountains), Nephelai (Clouds) and Potamoi (Rivers),

Theia

Theia (sometimes called Thia, Thea, Euryphaessa or Eurtphaessa) is the goddess of the moon. Theia was wedded to Hyperion (her sibling) and her children were: Helius ("Sun"), Eos ("Dawn") and Selene ("Moon"). She also was the mother of Cercopes by her other brother, Oceanus.

Phoebe

Phoebe was the goddess of the moon; through her marriage to her brother Coeus she bore Asteria and Leto. Through her daughter Leto, she became Apollo and Artemis' grandmother; and through Asteria she became the grandmother of Hekate. Phoebe was third in line to possess the reign of Delphi, which she eventually passed on to her grandson Apollo.

Themis

Initially the goddess of justice and Earth-goddess, Themis later became known as the goddess of justice and order. Themis was Zeus' second wife (who was also his aunt) and his first counselor. Often, she would be portrayed as the counselor of Zeus on matters of the rules of fate and divine law; in illustrations, she would be depicted sitting next to Zeus' throne. Themis had many offspring, including the Fates (Moerae), Seasons (Horae), Dike ("Justice"), Euriomia ("Order"), and Eirene ("Peace").

She witnessed Apollo's birth at Delos.

Mnemosyne

Mnemosyne (Mnemosyne) is the creator of words and language and the goddess of memory. She was called Moneta in Roman myths.

By her nephew Zeus, Mnemosyne was the mother of the nine Muses. For nine nights, Zeus slept with her. A year later, she welcomed her phenomenal daughters whom she named Urania, Polymnia, Calliope, Terpischore, Erato, Thaleia, Euterpe, Cleio and Melpomene.

CHAPTER III

The Twelve Olympians

The twelve major deities of the ancient Greek religion and its mythology were called the Olympians. After the toppling of the Titans, they ruled over every facet of human life. The Chief gods and goddesses were: Zeus, Apollo, Artemis, Dionysus, Demeter, Ares, Hera, Hermes, Athena, Poseidon, Hephaestus, and Aphrodite.

Other Olympian Gods

Although depicted as Olympians, the other deities were rather menials or functionaries of the chief Olympian gods. For instance, the Muses were owned by Apollo, the Horae by Zeus, the Erotes by Aphrodite and Eileithyia and Heba by Hera.

The Gods Categorized by their functions

The Olympian gods and their minions could be listed according to their functions. Below are some categories along with the gods.

The Theoi Agoraioi: These were the gods who presided over the "agora" (the people's assembly and the market place). Zeus—being the supreme leader—ruled over the people's assembly with Athena, Dike, Themis, and Calliope. Athena, Hermes, Hephaestus, and even

Apollo were the governors over the marketplace, presiding over potters, metalworkers, weavers, sculptors etc.

The Theoi Daitioi: Gods of the feasts and banquets, Dionysus and Hestia were accompanied by festive gods and the TheoiMovskoi in their reign.

The Theoi Gamelioi: These were deities who ruled over matters of marriage. The prominent deities of the reign were Zeus, Aphrodite and Hera; there were, however, many other gods.

The Theoi Georgikoi: They ruled over agrarian matters. Demeter was the supreme ruler but the chthonic gods were a dominant presence.

The Theoi Thesmioi: These were the deities of custom and divine law, over which Zeus Nomius (of the laws) and Demeter Thesmophorus (the law bringer) presided over. The rulers included the other rather subordinate gods such as Horae, Dike, Eunomia and others.

The Theoi Polemikio: The war of gods Ares and Athena were the forefront of leadership, joined by Enyo, Eris, Nike, Deimos and Phoebe. Zeus and Apollo also had certain wartime responsibilities.

The Theoi Montikoi: Apollo, Zeus and other oracle gods presided over divination, oracles and prophecy.

Zeus

The king of all the gods, the god of weather, sky, order and law — Zeus was styled "the father of gods and men".

He was a man with a sturdy stature; he had a dark beard. His common attributes were a thunderbolt, eagle, bull and royal scepter. His Roman name was Jupiter.

Before 265 BCE, Theocritus wrote this about Zeus: *Sometimes Zeus is clear, sometimes he rains*. This had to do with Zeus' power to control thunder, lightning and rain.

Zeus was the last child of Rhea and Cronus. He had five siblings: Demeter, Hestia, Poseidon, Hades and Hera. In fear of his children toppling him from his reign, Cronus took the extreme measure of swallowing his newborn children. He managed to consume his five offspring save Zeus.

Zeus was smuggled to Crete in a cave on Mount Dicte where he was suckled and raised by the divine goat Amaltheia.

After he had grown into a young man Zeus returned for retribution. He forced his father to regurgitate his siblings and spearheaded a triumphant uprising against the Titans in which he emerged as the victor. Once he had ascended to the throne he divided the universe amongst him and his brothers: Zeus took the heavens, Poseidon the sea and Hades the underworld.

Zeus was met with fierce challenges in his defense of the heavens. The attacks came from the children of Gaia— Gigantes, Typhon, and the twin brothers Aloadae. Zeus triumphed in all the battles and like he had done with the Titans he banished them to "Tartarus."

Zeus's list of liaisons

Zeus had almost innumerable liaisons who were deities, nymphs and mortals. Before his marriage to Hera, he consorted with quite a few of the female Titans. Here is the list of his spouses along with the children they bore him in chronological order.

1. Metis: As legend has it the goddess of prudence Metis, was Zeus' first love. She bore him Athena who Gaia warned would bear a daughter that would have a child who would usurp him from his throne. He took the preemptive measure—much like his father's—and ingested Metis and her unborn child. This was to follow up on the birth at close quarters. Hephaestus, the parthenogenetically son of Hera, split Zeus' head open from which a fully armed Athena emerged.

2. Themis: She was the Titaness goddess who bore him two sets of offspring: the three Horai (Seasons) and the three Moerae (fates).
3. Eurynome: She was the goddess who bore him the three Charites (graces) Aglaia, Euphrosyme and Thaleia.
4. Demeter: She was also his sibling who gave birth to white-armed Persephone.
5. Leto: This goddess bore him the twins Apollo and Artemis.
6. Hera: A sibling as well as a spouse, goddess Hera gave birth to Zeus' children Ares, Hebe and Eileithyia.

Zeus' list of lovers: Aegina, Protogenia, Alcmena, Himalia, Antiope, Hora, Asteria, Boetis, Calyce, Laodamia, Hera, Calliope, Othris, Callisto, Niobe, Hybris Carme, Danae, Demeter, Dia, Dino, Persephone Dione, Io Pandora Cassiopeia, Elare, Electra, Europa, Eurymedusa, Eurynome —and many more.

The offspring of Zeus

Among the many children of Zeus were Aphrodite, Selene, Hermes Athena, Pyrrha, Semele, Persephone Taygete, Apollo, Artemis, Themis, Heracles, Thyia, Dionysus, Ares and Hebe.

Athena

Athena (Minerva) was the goddess of counsel, war, heroic pursuits, the defense of towns weaving, pottery and many other crafts. In her depictions, she is a woman embellished with the monstrous head of

Gorgon, a crown with a crested helm and a snake-trimmed aegis cloak swathing her breast and arm. Athena would also be equipped with shield and spear.

Athena is known for her participation in the War of Giants where she plowed the Enkelados under Mount Etna and produced her aegis from the skinof Pallas.

Hephaestus, attempted rape on the goddess, but he failed and accidentally spilt his seed on the earth from which Erkhthonios was born. Athena adopted him and raised him as her own. As she was the virgin goddess, she had no biological offspring.

Athena sided for the Greeks in the Trojan War; she, however, turned on them and struck their ship with a storm when they failed to punish Oilean Ajax for his desecration of her Trojan shrine.

Apollo

One of the great divinities of the Greek Mythology, Apollo was the Olympian god of prophecy and oracles, plague, archery, sun and light and the protection of the young. His attributes are a laurel crown worn on his head, the lyre (or Cithara), his bow and arrows and, the most celebrated of them all, the tripod which symbolized his prophetic supremacy. The swan, wolf and dolphin are sacred to Apollo. He was a handsome, beardless young man with long hair.

He is the god of plague and he so happens to be the one who shot the arrows of plague in the campsite of the Greeks during the Trojan War, helping Paris slay Achilles.

He and his twin Artemis were the children of Zeus and Leto. His birth, much like his father's, was an interesting one. Although a wife to Zeus before his marriage to Hera, Leto was, nonetheless, considered a concubine and was later persecuted by Hera during her pregnancy. She wandered from pillar to post to give birth to her offspring but no one on earth offered refuge in fear of Hera's wrath. It was in the island of Delos—then a floating island—that Leto gave birth to Apollo. Her labour took nine days. Upon her request the floating island stood still on four pillars. The place came to be known as Asteria, and after the delivery of Apollo it was regarded as sacred. The death or birth of a human being was unlawful and thought a desecration; therefore, pregnant women were escorted to the neighboring island Rheneia to give birth.

Leto was unable to nurse Apollo after his birth so Themis provided him nectar and ambrosia. Having tasted the divine food, Apollo sprung up and requested for a lyre and a bow. He then declared to all of mankind the will of Zeus.

Apollo Slays the Serpent Python

During her pregnancy Leto was pursued by Python, the serpent appointed by Gaia (mother earth) to protect the oracular shrine of Delphi.

Often depicted as a male or female, Python nursed and consorted with Typhoeus, her brother. She was Gaia's child.

Apollo, four days after his birth, was able to avenge the dragon when he laid claim to the shrine. He slew Python with his arrow at mount Parnassus. As she withered in immense pain, Apollo stood above her and vaunted:

"Now rot here upon the soil that feeds man! You at least shall live no more to be a fell bane to men who eat the fruit of the all-nourishing earth, and who will bring hither perfect hecatombs. Against cruel death neither Typhoios [her consort] shall avail you nor ill-famed Khimaira [her spawn], but here, shall the Earth and shining Hyperion make you rot"

Apollo's action was not without consequences as he had slain the daughter/son of Gaia. He had to serve as a cowherd to king Admetus for nine years.

After the death of Python, Apollo took charge of the oracle, ridding the earth of the wrath that had befallen them during the reign of

Python who had destroyed crops, polluted streams and spring and sacked villages. He was later known as "Pythian Apollo." To Delphi (Pytho), he granted a bronze tripod and to the priestesses, "Pythia" being one, he dedicated divine powers.

Apollo Slays Tityos

Under the orders of Hera, Tityos (Tityus)—a Phokian giant—attempted to abduct the goddess Leto as she journeyed to Delphi. Apollo arrived at the scene and dealt with him using his golden sword and arrows. As a punitive measure Tityos was sent to the underworld to face eternal torment. There, he was anchored to the ground where two vultures feasted on his regenerating liver.

Apollo's Extensive Liaison

Like his father Zeus, Apollo had a great deal of relationships. The most famous of them were those with Daphne, Koronis, Kyrene and the Spartan prince Hyakinthos.

Divine Loves

Hestia: She was the goddess of hearth who Apollo and Poseidon vied for her love. Interestingly she declined them both and petitioned Zeus to permit her to sustain her virginity forever.

Mousai: It is said that Apollo sought after the nine muses and when the plan failed he chose to remain unmarried.

Durania: She was one of the nine Mousai who according to some accounts bore Apollo a child who was Linos.

Thaleia: (one of the nine Mousai) and Hekate (the goddess of Witchcraft) were amongst Apollo's divine loves.

Apollo's Mortal Loves (Women)

Apollo had a lot of mortal loves, among them being Hecuba the queen of Troy and wife of Priam. Troilius was born from this relationship. He was attacked and murdered by Achilles. Cassandra, daughter of Hecuba and Priam and Torilius' half-sister, was Apollo's love as well. She was seduced by his promise to teach her the craft of prophecy; however, once she had mastered the craft she betrayed him. Fueled by anger, Apollo declared Cassandra's prophecies invalid.

Apollo's other mortal lovers included: Akalle (Akakallis) the prince of Crete (Greek Aragon); Amphissa (Isse and Euboia) princess of Dryopia in central Greece; Hypermnestra, Queen of Argos in central Greece.

Apollo's Mortal loves (Men)

Adonis: A prince of Cyprus in eastern Mediterranean. Depicted as androgynous, he would share his affection as woman with Apollo and as a man with Aphrodite.

Hyakinthos (Hyacintus): A prince of Lakedaimenia in southern Greece, Hyakinthos was pursued by the two Gods Apollo and Zephyrus. His handsome and athletic features inflamed the amorous love of Apollo.

Apollo accidentally killed him in a game of quoits where he smashed his skull. The accident was brought about by Zephyrus who envied their love; he brewed an ill-wind which took the discus off course and had it land on Hyakinthos' head. Devastated by the accident, Apollo had a flower blossom in the area where his blood stained the earth; this was a token of love.

Other male loves of Apollo were Hymenaios (a prince of Magnesia and Kyparissos, the prince of Keos).

Apollo's Semi-divine Loves (Nymph)

Aithousa, a nymph of Boiotia; Akakollis, nymph of Krete; Melaina a Naias nymph of Phokis; Korykia a Naias nymph of Phokis—were but a few.

Apollo's infatuation with Daphne was Eros' doing. Provoked by Apollo's condescending remarks of his inferior archery skills and also irritated by his singing, Eros—the young god of love—invoked Apollo's obsession with the nymph Daphne. Whelmed by Apollo's incessant pursuit, Daphne fled to the mountains; he followed her there too. She was at her wits end when she asked Peneus, the river of god, for help. He transformed her into a laurel tree. The devastated Apollo turned the laurel into his consecrated tree.

From the many relationships Apollo had, a lot of children were born. The long list included Aristaeus, Asclepius, Troilus, Orpheus, Corybantes, Brankhos, Scylla, Idmon, Agreus, Amphiaraus,

Eleuther, Amphithemis, Apis, Chariclo, Anios, Delphos, Amphissos, Doros, Epidauros, Dryops, Eriopis, Erymanthos, Hilaera, Iamos, , Ismenos, Ileus, Laodokos, Keos, Coronos, Chairon, Lapiths, Cycnus, Centauros, Linos, The Leukippides, and Lykomedes.

Apollo's Destruction of the Niobides

Apollo could be destructive when he chose to be. When the mortal Niobe vaunted about her fourteen children (some accounts say six or seven) in front of Leto, saying that she was superior to her for she had bore more children than her (Leto had two). Apollo was vexed. He killed her sons and Artemis slew Niobe's daughters. Niobe, inundated by sorrow, changed into stone.

Apollo's Music Contest with Satyr Marsyas

Satyr Marsyas challenged Apollo to a music contest. Exasperated at this insistence, Apollo took up on the challenge and surfaced as the victor. He had Marsyas flayed alive for his audacity of challenging a god.

Artemis

The twin sister of Apollo, Airtimes (Diana) was the goddess of childbirth, hunting, wilderness, wild animals, and the protectress of the girl child until she reaches the age of marriage. Zeus and Leto were her parents.

Artemis was the virgin goddess who bore no children.

Apollo and Artemis would summon death and disease. She would target the female mass while he would be responsible for the male mass.

The simulacra of Artemis would be a girl dressed in short knee-length chiton with an armor of a hunting bow and quiver of arrows. She would also be escorded by stags or hunting dogs.

The goddess was severely beaten by Hera in the fuming conquest of the gods during the Trojan War.

Aphrodite

Aphrodite (Venus) was the goddess of love, beauty, procreation and pleasure. In accordance with the cosmogonic descriptions of her, "she was the epitome of generative powers of nature and the mother of all living things".

In her depiction, she would often be accompanied by Eros (the young god of love). Dove, apple, mirror and scallop shells were her attributes. When depicted in classical sculpture and fresco, she would be nude.

According to Hesiod's account it is said that Aphrodite was conceived from the genitals of Ouranos in the sea's foam; however, according to Homer Iliad, she is believed to be the child of Zeus.

It is believed that Aphrodite was married to Hephaestus, but her infidelity was quite profuse; among her many affairs were those with Ares, Dionysus, Adonis, Hermes and Poseidon. During her affair with Ares, Hephaestus trapped both of them in a net.

From her relationships were bore Priapus, Bacchus, Rhodos, Herophilus and others.

Demeter

The goddess of agriculture, bread and grain, Demeter (Ceres) was one of the great Olympians. She ruled over the prominent Mystery Cults that guaranteed a blessed afterlife to its initiates. She was one of the five siblings of Zeus – daughter of Rhea and Cronus.

She consorted with Iasion, Zeus, Oceanus, Karmanor, Poseidon and Triptolemus.

Demeter was the mother of Persephone,Arion, Plutus, Despoina,Eubuleus,Philomelus, Chrysothemis and Amphitheus I.

In her depictions, Demeter was a mature woman holding sheaves of wheat and a torch. She would often wear a crown.

She brought down great dearth on the earth in the wake of her daughter Persephone's abduction by Hades—her brother.

Dionysus

Dionysus (Fufluns) was the great god of wine, vegetation, pleasure and festivity. There were often two kinds of depiction of Dionysus. He would either be portrayed as a beautiful feminine man with long hair or an older man with beards. He would often be accompanied by a troop of female devotees or nymphs (Satyrs and Mainades).

His parents were Rhea and Cronus.

His attributes included the drinking cup, the thyrsus, leopard and fruiting vine.

Hera

Primarily the deity of women, children, family and marriage, Hera was also the goddess of the sky and starry heavens. To the Romans she was known as Juno. She was both the sister and wife of Zeus from whom she bore Hebe, Ares and Eileithyia. Her other children were Hephaestus and Eris.

She was illustrated as a gorgeous woman wearing a crown and holding a royal, lotus tipped staff. At times she would be represented with a royal lion in her hands, or would have a cuckoo or hawk as her like.

Her rage emanating from the jealousy of Zeus' affairs led to her bearing Hephaestus parthenogenetically.

The Judgment of Paris

The judgment of Paris was instigated by the wedding ceremony of Thetis and Peleus. All the gods but Eris, the goddess of discord, were invited. She appeared at the festivity anyway, but she was asked to leave. In anger, she cast a golden apple bearing inscription 'For the Fairest' amongst the goddesses. Aphrodite, Hera, and Athena laid claim to the apple. Zeus was called upon to mediate so he requested Hermes take them to Paris of Troy to settle the argument. The three goddesses had to stand before the judgment of the shepherd prince. They cajoled him with gift for favor. In the end, the prince chose Aphrodite who proposed to him his most prized desire: Helen as his bride. Shortly after, Helen was abducted and this led to

Poseidon

Poseidon (Neptune) was the god of sea, rivers, drought, flood, earthquakes and horses. He was represented as a mature man of sturdy stature with a dark beard and a trident in his hands. The child of Cronus and Rhea, he was one of the siblings of Zeus swallowed by his father and later regurgitated.

He consorted with Aphrodite. His children were, Polyphemus, Triton, Belus, Atlas, Agenor, Neleus.

In the War of the Titans, Poseidon was the partner of Hades and Zeus in the imprisonment of the deities in Tartaros.

In the division of the universe amongst the Cronuses, he was granted the rule of the sea. He resided in the depth of the sea adjacent to Aegae in Euboea where he kept his horses with brazen hoofs and golden manes.

He and Apollo built the walls of Troy for Laomedon; however, after the construction of the walls Laomedon refused to present the gods with the mandatory rewards. Poseidon avenged by sending a marine monster on the Trojans.

He seduced many women includingAithra, Tyro, Amymone, and the Gorgon Medusa.

Hermes

Hermes (Mercury) was the god of many things: animal husbandry, roads, travel, hospitality, heralds, trade, language, writing, thievery, persuasion, astrology, cunning wiles, gymnasium athletic competitions, astrology, astronomy and diplomacy. He was the offspring of Maia and Zeus.

Hermes was depicted as either an older man with beards or a young beardless man, handsome and athletic. Herald's wand (caduceus), winged sandals (talaria), lyre, rooster, tortoise and at times a winged cap and cloak were his attributes.

His children were Pan, Hermaphroditus, Abderus, Autolycus, Tyche and Angelia; and his consorts included Hecate (wife), Merope, Aphordite, Peith and Dryope.

Hephaestus

Hephaestus (Vulcan) was the parthenogenetic son of Hera and the god of fire, stonemasonry, metalworking and the craft of sculpture.

He was represented as a bearded man with hammer and tongs in his hand and ridding a donkey.

He consorted with Aphrodite and Aglaea; his offspring include Thalia, Eucleai, Euphme, Philophrosyne, Cabeiri, and Euthenia.

Hephaestus was famous for his participation in the birth of Athena, and his attempted rape on her. From this failed assault resulted the impregnation of Earth and the birth of Erikhthonios.

Ares

Ares (Mars) was the god of war, civil order and courage. The paintings of Greek art depict him as either a bearded warrior armored and equipped with weaponry or a nude beardless young man carrying a spear and a helm. His parents were Hera and Zeus.

Ares is perhaps most famous for his adulterous affair with Aphrodite and the slaying of Adonis who vied for his mistress' affection.

CHAPTER IV

The Heroes

What gave Greek mythology the life and the exuberant colors that continue to marvels the world, are its heroes and heroines. The imagination that went into the crafting of their traits, lives, and the daring adventures upon which they embarked and triumphed are part of what makes Greek mythology ever so more fascinating, and what basically helped it survive for so long a time.

Amongst the greatest and most celebrated heroes in Greek mythology are *Achilles*, *Heracles*, *Odysseus*, *Hector* and *AjaxtheGreat.*

Heracles

Heracles or Hercules, as the Romans called him, is perhaps the most renowned heroes in Greek mythology. Hercules was a hero most celebrated for the enormous strength he possessed and the daring adventures he courageously challenged, mainly the completion of 12 nearly impossible labors. The world never seems to grow tired of hearing the endless stream of stories of this hero; even in the 21st century, his name still has a vast presence, which in some way makes him all the more immortal.

He was the son of the mortal Alcmene and the all mighty god Zeus. With the supernatural strength he inherited from his father, Hercules was never a normal child. But what predestined him to a life filled with challenges was when he drank the milk of the Queen of the Gods, Hera, at his birth.

When Hera realized the strength and origin of the baby, she instantly became his arch nemesis. And as her first attempt to eliminate him, she sent out a snake to strangle him in his cradle. But it wasn't much of a labor for baby Hercules to strangle and kill the snake with his feeble hands.

Hercules then grew up and began to face far graver challenges in life, most of which Hera crafted herself. Amongst the most famous adventures of Hercules are the Twelve Labors he performed and his slaying of the fire-breathing giant, Cacus, in Palatine Hill (a site where Rome was later built).

According to legends, Cacuslived in a cave situated in a distant area on the Aventine, where Hercules resided with the cattle he had brought from Geryon. Cacus fell fond of these cattle and when Hercules fell asleep at night, Cacus stole eight of them and took them to his cave by dragging them by the tail (or by making them walk backwards to leave a false trail —according to other legends).

Infuriated, Hercules then set out to attack Cacus, who did whatever was possible to block Hercules out of the cave. But Hercules found his entrance and started to attack the beast. Cacus tried defending himself by gushing out fire and smoke, but Hercules found his ways around and managed to get hold of Cacus and strangle him to death. And for this heroic feat, Hercules was worshiped.

The Twelve Labors was the grave consequence of one of Hera's crafty plots. According to legends, Hercules suffered from epilepsy, and when he was going through one of his seizures, Lussa, the Goddess of Madness, entered his body and Hera managed to drive him mad. As a result of his madness, Hercules ended up killing his family.

To make amends for this unpardonable deed, Hercules had to perform 12 nearly impossible labors.

1. Slay the Nemean Lion.
2. Slay the nine-headed Lernaean Hydra.
3. Capture the Golden Hind of Artemis.
4. Capture the Erymanthian Boar.
5. Clean the Augean stables in a single day.
6. Slay the Stymphalian Birds.
7. Capture the Cretan Bull.
8. Steal the Mares of Diomedes.
9. Obtain the girdle of Hippolyta, Queen of the Amazons.
10. Obtain the cattle of the monster Geryon.
11. Steal the apples of the Hesperides.
12. Capture and bring back Cerberus.

Achilles

"Sing, Goddess, of the rage of Peleus' son Achilles, the accursed rage that brought great suffering to the Achaeans." — Iliad.

Achilles is known for being the fiercest warrior, the hero that triumphed in the Trojan War. He was the offspring of Peleus, king of the Myrmidons, and Thetis, the nymph. According to the legends, Thetis' hand was pursued by both Zeus and Poseidon. But when the fore-thinker, Prometheus, prophesied that Thetis was going to have a son destined to be mightier than his father, their quest ended abruptly, and Thetis tied the knot with Peleus.

In the attempt to render Achilles immortal Thetis, held him by the leg and dipped him in the river Styx. But his heel –the part by which his mother held him and that wasn't submerged –became defenseless.

There were quite a lot of events in the Trojan War that magnified Achilles' greatness. But the one that exceeded all was his fight against Hector, the brave Trojan leader, which took place before the Gates of Troy.

What instigated the combat was the killing of Achilles' most cherished companion and Nestor's son, Patroclus. When the Trojans charged at the Greek army and managed to push them back towards the beaches, Patroclus, dreading the defeat of his comrades assembled the Myrmidons and went into battle with the Trojans wearing Achilles' armor. Patroclus did manage to push the Trojans back, but it wasn't long before he was defeated and killed by the Trojan leader, Hector.

Following the news of this tragedy, Achilles was swamped with a rage that seemed even beyond the control of the Gods, even his mother's plea had but very little effect on him, "My son, if you avenge the death of your friend Patroclus, and kill Hector, you yourself shall die; for straightway, after Hector, is death appointed unto you." –

Homer's Iliad.

Achilles fueled with rage, went after Hector to avenge Patroclus's death, and after a couple of challenges, he was finally able to have the battle he so desperately wanted with Hector.

According to the legends, Hector charged at Achilles with his sword but missed. Then falling at his feet, Hector begs for his body to be spared the degradation after his death. But Achilles responded *"my rage, my fury would drive me now to hack your flesh away and eat you raw – such agonies you have caused me"*.

After Hector's death, the Trojans joined forces with the Queen of the Amazons, Penthesilea, and the King of Ethiopians, Memnon, to defend the city. Achilles ended up killing them both. But then Paris, the Trojan prince who caused the Trojan War, ended up killing Achilles by shooting him with an arrow on his most vulnerable spot – his heel.

Odysseus

The Trojan War was certainly an event that accommodated a lot of heroes. And Achilles was definitely one of them, but there were also other worthy conquerors, such as Odysseus, whose partaking in this war was of extreme significance.

Odysseus is the doyen in Homer's epic poem *Odysseus.* He is the king of Ithaca and, according to various sources, the son of Laertes and Anticlea. Odysseus was married to Penelope and with her he fathered a son named Telemachus.

His participation in the Trojan War had a rather interesting beginning. At first Odysseus didn't want take part in the quest to siege Troy, and to evade it he faked his own insanity. But then Palamedes, suspecting the validity of his claim, drew out his sword and threatened to kill his son. At that juncture, Odysseus confessed and joined the expedition.

In the Trojan War Odysseus was known as the crafty hero. He was given this title for his disguised entrance into Troy and for coming up with the wooden horse, an entity that tipped the balance for the Greeks.

Odysseus' magnificent journey of life, however, didn't end at the Trojan War. When Polyphemus, Poseidon's Cyclops son, killed and feasted on some of Odysseus' men, he, with the help of his crew, managed to get the one eyed giant drunk and blinded him with a sharp stake.

Outraged by his deed, Poseidon condemned him to a decade long journey before he could go back home to Ithaca. His journey was filled with dangerous adventures in hostile lands and violent seas.

'And…I saw Iphimedeia the wife of Aloeus, who said that Poseidon lay with her, and so she bare twin sons, that were but short-lived. Tallest they were of all that the fertile earth nurtured, and goodliest by far, next to famous Orion; nine years old were they, and nine cubits was their breadth, but in height they were nine fathom. And they twain threatened to arouse the din of furious battle even against the gods in Olympos. Ossa they were minded to pile upon Olympos, and on Ossa, Pelion with its waving forests, that the heavens might be climbed; and this they had accomplished, if they had come to the measure of their full growth; but the son of Zeus, whom LetoFairlocks brought forth, destroyed them both, before the down blossomed beneath their temples and their cheeks were covered with the bloom of a young beard.'

– Excerpt from Homer's *Odysseus.*

Hector and Ajax the Great

Ajax, otherwise known as Aias, was amongst the fiercest Greek warriors that took part in the Trojan War as the leader of the Salamis forces. He is duly noted for his epic duel with Hector.

Ajax is the offspring of King Telamon and Periboea, and cousin of Achilles. He is known for his enormous size, strength and courage, which was considerably displayed in his duel with Hector.

There were two instances where the Greek hero Ajax and the Trojan hero Hector met in the battleground. The first combat took place when Hector asked for the fighting to cease and for the Greeks to issue forth their bravest warrior to face him in a deadly combat. The Greeks agreed and Ajax was, by a quirk of fate, chosen as Hectors contender.

The duel was long and ferocious; both were worthy opponents, and at the end no winner was praised and no looser was condemned. It ended with the adversaries exchanging gifts; Ajax gave Hector a purple sash and Hector handed Ajax his sword.

Their next encounter was when Hector and his army advanced on the Greeks at the Mycenaean camp. When the Trojans attacked the Greek ships, Ajax threw a giant rock at Hector and almost killed him. Hector made a quick recovery, and with the absence of Achilles, the Trojans were able to further their attack, to a point of incinerating their vessels. And until additional Greek troops arrived, who were led by Patroclus, Ajax practically fought them off single handedly.

Ajax wasn't just Achilles' cousin but also his closest companion and when Achilles was killed Ajax was the one that brought his body and armor home while Odysseus resisted the Trojans.

Achilles' armor then later caused a dispute that eventuated in Ajax's death. Both Ajax and Odysseus claimed this armor. But the Greeks voted for Achilles' armor to be in the possession of Odysseus. Ajax, angered by the results, then decides to retaliate and attack the Greek troops at night.

But then Athena, the Goddess of Wisdom, intervenedand clouded his mind and vision leading him to slaughter a flock of sheep instead. When he gained consciousness, Ajax, ashamed of what he did, ended up killing himself with the sword given to him by Hector.

CHAPTER V

The Trojan War

As legend has it, The Trojan War was declared against the city of Troy in Asia Minor by Achaeans' armies after the elopement (or kidnapping) of Helen of Sparta by Paris of Troy. It was also a way for Zeus to depopulate the world.

The Trojan prince Paris (also named Alexandros) was appointed by Zeus to decide who among the three goddesses Hera, Athena and Aphrodite should win the prize for beauty. The goddesses endeavored to bribe Paris: Athena offered him wisdom, skill in battle and the capacity of the greatest warriors; Hera presented him political influence and control of all of Asia; and Aphrodite promised him a wife that's known to be the beautiful woman in the whole of the universe— Helen. Paris couldn't resist Aphrodite's offer and abducted Helen, causing the Trojan War.

The Greek Forces

King Agamemnon of Mycenae was the leader of the allied Archaians or Greek armies. The represented regions or cities were Euboea, Boiotia, Argos, Athens, Phocia, Sparta, Kephalopnia, Rhodes, Arcadia, the Cyclades, Magnesia, Crete and Corinth. Homer asserts that there were 'tens of thousands' of armies.

There were some great heroes amongst the Greek warriors who have displayed tremendous valor on the battlefield. Amongst the crucial were: Odysseus, Achilles, Diomedes, Ajax, Patroclus, Menestheus and Idomenus.

The Greek army was supported by most of the Olympian gods. According to Homer, Athena, Hera, Poseidon, Hermes, Hephaistos and Thetis extended their support to the Greeks directly or indirectly. Some favored warriors fighting on Troy were given protection by the gods who would do such things as deflect the spears that were directed towards them or spirit them away to a safe place when there is too much heat and blood in the battle.

The Trojan Army

With King Priam as leader, the Trojan army safeguarding the city of Troy received quite a lot of help from various allies. Amongst them were: Halizones, Carians, Kaukones, Lycians, Kikones, Maionians, Paionians, Pelasgians, Paphlagonians, Mysians and Thracians.

The Trojans, as well, had their own heroes including Priam's son, Hektor, Sarpedon, Aeneas, Phorkys, Glaukos, Rhesos and Poulydamas. The Trojans too, had Gods that worked in their favor during the battle— Apollo, Ares, Leto and Aphrodite sided with the Trojans.

Battles

The prolonged siege and the city's laudable ability to withstand the intruders for an extended time, chiefly due to its robust fortifications, was what defined most parts of the Trojan War. In Greek mythology it is stated that Apollo and Poseidon where the ones who built the strong walls of Troy.

Apollo and Poseidon, as a consequence of their irreverence, were sentenced to serve Laomedon, the Trojan King, for one year. There were, however, armies engaging in a fight beyond the walls of the city, mostly by an army on foot employing swords and spears. They would protect themselves by holding a shield, wearing an armor and helmet.

Over the years, wars were waged across the regions of Troy; nevertheless the most riveting events in the battles seem to have been saved for when the siege was nearing its concluding year. Below are selections of the most prominent parts.

Menelaus vs. Paris

Due to the indecisive battles, Menelaus proposed to battle Paris in a single-combat to bring the war to a peaceful end. Paris agreed and they drew lots to witness who would be the first to throw the spear. Paris hurled first and won, however his spear disembarked innocuously in Menelaos' shield. Then, the Greek king, with outstanding force, threw his spear which went through Paris' shield and ended up piercing his armor. If it was for that sway at that brief moment, Paris would have been slain.

Nevertheless, Menelaus did not complete his mission; he swung his sword and struck a dreadful blow on Paris' helmet. The sword, nonetheless, shattered and became one with the dust. Then Menelaus firmly grasped the prince's helmet started to drag him around the field. But then Aphrodite intervened and Paris was saved. She broke the strap of helmet around his neck which was causing him to chock, covered him in a thick mist and helped him escape death.

Hektor vs. Ajax

The duel between the two great heroes resembles that of Menelaus and Paris. Both of them threw their spear but with no achievement. Hektor then hurls a huge rock at Ajax, which he repelled with his shield. In return, Ajax threw an even larger rock shattering Hector's shield. The fight was put to an end by both their comrades after Hektor and Ajax withdrew their swords and settled for a mortal combat, as it was dawning. In respect to the code of honor, the even bid their farewell amicably by offering gifts to one another; Ajax gave a superb purple belt and Hektor gave him a silver-hilted sword.

The Greek Camp Ambushed

Following a vigorous day of battle, Hector with his Trojan army managed to assault the walls of the Greek campsite. The Trojans then smashed through the gates and the Greeks were forced to retreat back to their ships. However, Poseidon encouraged the assembled Greeks and they somehow managed to draw back the Trojans. Then with the assistance of Apollo, Hektor, yet again, drove the Greeks back to their ships where he intended to set them in flames and demolish them once and for all.

Death of Patroclus

For most parts of the war, Achilles, one of the greatest warriors in Greece, chose to play a rather neutral role. Achilles refused to re-join the conflict even upon many requests. But when the Greek camp was under attack, Patroclus pleaded for Achilles, his great friend and mentor, to join the battle. Achilles declined then Patroclus asked asked to wear Achilles' amour so that he could lead the Myrmidons himself. When Achilles saw the burning of one of the Greek ships, he reluctantly bestowed his approval. He cautioned Patroclusto only to drive the Trojans away from the campsite and not to pursue them all to the walls of Troy.

Patroclusthen led the Greek to fight back. Assuming it was Achilles himself, the Trojans recoiled in disorder and Patroclus was even able to slaughter Sarpedon, the great Trojan hero. The young Patroclusamidst the successful battle disregarded Achilles' earnest counsel and continued the fight towards Troy. Nonetheless, in that moment, Apollo, in support of the Trojans interceded and hit the helmet and armor from Patroclus, broke his spear asunder and whacked his shield away from his arm. The unprotected and exposed Patroclus was then severely wounded by Euphorbos and then Hektor callously stabbed him with his own spear.

Achilles Resumes Battle

Achilles, on hearing of the death of his good friend, went nearly mad. He was overpowered by grief and he swore to avenge Hektor and the Trojans for it. After mourning, Achilles at last decided to engage in the battlefield once more.

Achilles, with his new magnificent armor which his mother persuaded Hephaistos to create, utterly routed the Trojans the next day.

Achilles vs. Hektor

Hektor stood alone outside the walls; but the glimpse of the threatening and powerful Achilles in rage made him run for shelter. Achilles nevertheless chased Hektor around the walls of the city, three times, to be specific. Hektor finally was caught by Achilles and was killed with a vicious stab with a spear in his throat. Achilles returned to camp, dragging the body behind his chariot. This was an utterly dishonorable act —against all rules and regulations of ancient warfare.

Funeral games were held over Patroclus. Meanwhile, Priam came secretly to Achilles by night to ask for the return of his son's corpse so as to at least give him an appropriate burial. At first, Achilles was reluctant, the old man's plea however, managed to convince Achilles and he allowed the release of the body. The *Iliad* ends with his funeral, the war though, still had quite a whole lot more tales to tell.

Victory & the Wooden Horse

The Trojan War entailed several more exiting series including Achilles' battle and murder of Memnon, the Ethiopian King. Achilles himself was executed by an arrow shot either by Paris, or by Apollo (disguised as Paris, in some accounts). Odysseus and Ajax quarreled over this astounding armor and Ajax lost. Ruled by disappointment and rage for losing, he went into rampage and slaughtered a flock of sheep which he considered to be Greeks. Ajax then fell on his own sword killed himself.

Achilles' son, Philokteles, in retaliation for his father's death, gravely shot Paris with the celebrated bow of Hercules. At last, Odysseus disguised himself and entered the city. He then managed to steal the sacred Palladion statue of Athena.

The conclusion of the war came with one final plan. Motivated by Athena, Odysseus formulated a new ruse— a giant hollow wooden horse, an animal that was sacred to the Trojans. It was a gigantic wooden horse constructed by Epeius which concealed Greek armies within. Sinon, a Greek spy, convinced the Trojans that the horse was a present from the Greeks. The Trojans accepted the horse as a peace offering as they were understandably elated and celebrating their victory. Meanwhile, the Greek armies mounted out of the wooden horse and bolted the walls of the city for their fellow soldiers to enter. The city was then utterly ransacked and the peopled were either slain or enslaved.

Owing to their merciless destruction of the city and its people— the blasphemous deeds such as rape of Cassandra being one gruesome event— the gods started to take punitive measures against the Greeks. They sent heavy storms to destroy their ships and those who have returned were first forced to undergo a prolonged and incredibly difficult journeys.

Ten Little Known Facts about Greek Mythology

Zeus' Dirty Secret

Zeus was as mighty as that of his title, God of all Gods. And he had quite a lot of secrets, but not all of them were pure and chaste, some were mind bogglingly dirty.

Ever wonder why Zeus is the father of so many heroes and Gods, yes, well that's because he was, as some might call him, a serial rapist. According to legends, Zeus had an unforgiving weakness for both mortal and immortal women. And he used his mighty powers to take advantage of them and fulfill his desires.

Zeus would often transmute himself into an animal to woo and advance on the ones he was attracted to. For instance, he transformed in to an eagle and wooed Asteria and Aigina; as a serpent he had his way with Demeter and her daughter, Persephone; as a Swan he advanced on Leda, with whom he fathered the most beautiful woman on earth, Helen of Troy; as a goat he wooed Boetis, and let's just say that the list goes on and on. He would also lead women to believe that he was their husband, as in the case of Hercules's mother, Alkmene.

Good Guy Hades

How could anyone feel anything besides the pervasion of a bloodcurdling sensation, when Hades, the God of Death and the Underworld, is mentioned? He is simply terrifying and his title certainly works to further magnify the horror and darkness that defines his being. Hades doesn't have many good deeds to claim, surprisingly, however, he wasn't ALL bad, especially for a God of Death and the Underground.

First of all, it wasn't Hades' choice to be the ruler of the Underground; he was relegated to this realm when he and his brothers, Poseidon and Zeus, agreed to draw straws and decide upon who was to rule which realm. Zeus got the Upper world, Poseidon the Seas, and Hades the Underworld.

As ruler of the Underworld, Hades wasn't as diabolical; he was actually fair and helpful at times. One instance was when Hercules, in performance of one of his 12 labors, approached Hades and asked to go back to the upper world with his three headed dogs. Another was when Orpheus, in seek of recovering his bride from the underworld, approached Hades and pleaded for her release. Hades agreed to let his bride go but only under the condition that he doesn't look back.

It should also be noted that, contrary to what many believe, the ones who decided upon the fate of souls are the three demigods, Minos, Aiakos, and Rhadamanthys, and not Hades.

The Birth of Athena

As it was earlier touched upon, the birth of Athena was rather fascinating. Metis, the Titan Goddess of Wisdom and mother of Athena, was Zeus' lover. But when he learned of Gaia's prophecy that Metis was going to bear a child that would be greater than its father, one who would gain the lordship of the sky, Zeus swallowed her and her unborn child.

Metis then gave birth to Athena in Zeus' belly. Then one day, Zeus came down with a terrible headache, and asked Prometheus, Hephaestus, Hermes, and Ares to cut open his skull with an axe.

When Zeus' skull was cut open, the fully grown Athena leaped out.

Athena, Guardian of Athens

Athena otherwise known as Pallas Athena is celebrated for being the most beautiful guardian Goddess of Athens with thousands of grey eyes. However, her stand and reign over Athens was something she had to fight for with the God of the seas, Poseidon.

To settle the dispute between Athena and Poseidon, as to who should become the guardian of the city, they agreed to let the occupants decide. To win favors, Poseidon gave the city water, which was salty and thus disliked. And Athena gave them an olive tree, hence her title 'the Grey—Eyes Goddess'. The people chose her as their guardian, for her offering proved to be more beneficial.

The Story of Adonis, Aphrodite's Lover

Adonis' life story and his love affair with Aphrodite is a count of so many interesting events. And it all began when the Goddess of Love and Beauty, Aphrodite, decided to punish the King of Cyprus, Cyniras, for publicly saying that his daughter's beauty was far greater than Aphrodite's.

She foisted upon his daughter, Myrrha, an irrepressible lust for her father. Myrrha then started to pursue her father, but was always rejected by him. Then one day she disguised herself as a prostitute and had her way with him. She eventually got pregnant and when her father discovered the truth, he charged at her with a knife. Myrrha then ran out of the house and prayed for the Gods to grant her mercy. The Gods heard her prayer and turned her into a myrrh tree or balsam.

As a tree, Myrrha gave birth to a baby boy, which Aphrodite found as she was passing by. Aphrodite took pity on the abandoned child and sent him to Hades to be raised by Persephone. The child then grew up to be the handsome Adonis, who later became Aphrodite's lover.

The Mother of Monsters

Daughter of Phorcys and Ceto, Echinda was half-woman and half-serpent. She was the sister of Medusa and Geryon and the wife of Typhon, a hundred-headed dragon. They were the parents of several famous and horrifying monsters: Nemean lion, Hydra, Cerberus and Ladon. Her children included, Chimaira, the Sphinx, Scylla the sea monster, the Colchian dragon and eagle that visited Prometheus daily to eat his liver as his everlasting penalty for thieving fire from the gods.

Aphrodite's Military Side

Aphrodite, daughter of Zeus and Goddess of love, beauty and marriage, was also known and worshiped as the Goddess of war.

As evidenced by the statues of armed and accoutered Aphrodite recovered from several port cities, she was certainly recognized for her military might. And her long lasting love affair with Ares, the God of War, serves as more evidence.

From Ares she gave birth to four children – Eros, Deimos, Anteros, Harmonia, and Phobos. And so in many ways, her involvement in warlike affairs was quite inevitable.

"Taking the bull by its horns"

"Taking the bull by its horns" is a popular phrase that society most commonly uses. And guess what? It happens to be the produce of Greek Mythology.

Of the 12 labors Hercules had to perform as a punishment for the morbid crime he committed on his wife and children, one was to capture the Cretan Bull. His task was to grab the bull by its horns and rescue the city of Crete from its destruction. He successfully accomplished this mission and that resulted in the saying "Taking the bull by its horns" taking root.

Atlas Punishment

Atlas was punished by Zeus to hold up the sky on his shoulder for infinity after the Titans were defeated in the war against Zeus. Atlas managed to make Hercules hold it up for him, ephemeral it was however, as Hercules tricked him to holding the weight of the heavens again. He is erroneously depicted to be holding up the earth.

Theseus the Terrible

Theseus in Greek mythology is the brave hero that slew Minotaur, defeated the Amazons, and rescued Persephone from the Underground. But there are some things about this hero that are not so laudable; in fact they're terrible.

One of Theseus' greatest feats was entering the Labyrinth and slaying the Minotaur. But this was an impossible task to complete, one that would've claimed his life had it not been for the help of King Minos'daughter, Ariadne. But after all that she had done for him, he waited for her to fall asleep and abandoned her in the island of Naxos.

Another one of Theseus' dirty deeds was when he founded the city of Athens and decided to populate his newfound city by raping the women.

Pandora: The First Mortal Women

According to Greek mythology, Pandora was the first mortal woman. She was created by Zeus for the purpose of avenging Prometheus for stealing fire from the Gods.

All the Gods and Goddess presented her with a special gift; Hephaestus formed her out of wet clay; Athena gave her life and clothed her; the Charites and Peitho embellished her with jewelry; Aphrodite gave her beauty and charm; the Horae festooned her with flowers, and Hermes taught her the ways and how's of treachery and guile.

Pandora, now fully formed, was then presented to Epimetheus, Prometheus' brother, as a gift from Zeus. Prometheus warned his brother not to accept any gift from Zeus, but Epimetheus, enthralled by Pandora's beauty couldn't do anything but accept her.

As a wedding present, Zeus gave Pandora a box and told her never to open it. Flooded by curiosity, Pandora then did what she is most famous for in Greek Mythology— she opened the box and released the evils in the world.

NORSE MYTHOLOGY

Norse Mythology is one of the most fascinating relics of history that needs no exaltation. Its multi-faceted features are enough to pique the interest of even the unwavering skeptics. This eBook discusses at length the mesmerizing gods, their enigmatic and at times discreditable characters and deeds; the ferocious giants, elves, dwarves and heroes; the nine worlds and much more.

The book embodies the sentiment of the indigenous religion of Northern Europe and touches upon some of the practices pertinent to the Gods. Imbued with the most enthralling facts, this eBook will not only rivet you but also edify you, giving you great insights.

There is also the bonus chapter which is quite the reservoir of intriguing facts known to precious little.

CHAPTER I

Norse Mythology

Norse Mythology, also called Scandinavian mythology is a kind of religion that was practiced by the people of Scandinavian countries (Denmark, Sweden and Norway) and people from the Northern parts of Germany. The myths give a clear picture of a universe which involved the battles that had transpired between the gods and giants in a cosmic conflict destined to end in the annihilation of the world. Several gods are mentioned in the Norse Mythology such as: *Thor*: a fierce and valiant god who relentlessly pursues his foes and crushes them; *Odin*: god of battle, wisdom and poetry; *Njoror*: a provider of wealth and land, and much more (the different deities will be elaborately dilated on in the following chapters.)

The Norse Mythology stems from the myths and legends of northern peoples who spoke Germanic language. Its many features resemble that of the pre-Christian Germanic groups' mythology. The myth followed some of the groups who migrated to England and Scandinavia. As they converted to Christians, their traditional beliefs began to recede. In Scandinavia, nevertheless, Christianity did not pervade until a later date, and Germanic mythology – of the Norse version— had an iron grip throughout the Viking era, from about A.D. 750 to 1050.

The world of Norse mythology consists of two groups of gods: the Æsirand the Vanir, as well as giants, elves, dwarfs, trolls, and heroic

The Æsir: they were the gods of the sky and war. Amongst the chief were Odin (considered the ruler of the deities and the creator of humans by the Vikings), the mighty Thor (second most important Norse deity), Baldur (Balder or Baldr), Loki and many more.

The Vanir: the Vanir were associated with fertility, the earth and prosperity. At first, Vanir and Æsir waged war against each other, but after realizing that neither side could triumph, the two groups of gods made peace. Together they battled their mutual enemy— the giants. To secure eternal peace, some of the Vanir came to Asgard, home to Æsir, as hostages; among them were Njord with his twin children Freyr and Freya.

CHAPTER II

Gods and Goddesses

The Norse mythology is painted with a legion of mesmerizing deities.

The Æsir tribes were the main deities that ruled over the cosmos and maintained order. Among them were: Odin, Thor, Baldur, Tyr, Frigg, Höðr, Heimdall, Idun, Bragi, Fjorgyn and Fjorgynn, Sif, Ve and Vili, Jord, Forseti, Mani and Sol.

The **Vanir** gods and goddesses were the second tribes of deities. They were more involved in the natural world than the Æsirtribes. Among the Vanir were Freya, Freyr, Njord, Nerthus, Odr and Gullveig.

Borr

Little account is given of Borr (or Burr) in the literary sources but he was the offspring of Buri who was the first of the Æsir tribes. Borr was married to the daughter of Bolthorn, Bestla who bore him the half-god, half-giants Odin, Vili and Vi. Together, the siblings slew Ymir—the first of the god like giants—and from his corpse they created the world: from his blood the oceans emerged, vegetation from his hair, the soil from his skin and muscles, clouds floated out from his brains, and from his skull the sky was formed.

Odin

Perhaps one of the most enigmatic and colorful characters in the relics of world literature, Odin (pronounced OH-din) was the all-knowing, all-father of the Gods and Lord of *Asgard*. In the Old Norse language he was known as *óðinn*; in Old Saxon and Old English, *Woden*; in High Germanic, *Wuton, Wotan or Wodan*.

He was the chief of Æsir and the god of war, death and knowledge. Odin enjoyed an all-round reign which governed over matters of death, royalty, healing, the gallows, royalty, sorcery, battle, frenzy, knowledge and the runic alphabet.

Odin is the son of Borr (Burr) and Bestla—one of the first frost-giants. His relationships included Frigg, Jörð (the earth) Skaði, Rindr and Gunnlöð. According to the Eddic poems, the skaldic poems and others, Odin is the father of Thor, Baldur (Baldr or Balder), Viðarr and Váli. However, according to the literary works of SnorriSturluson, Odin has fathered all the gods.

Despite him being the leader of Æsir and the lord of Asgard, Odin had a penchant for distant and solitary travels. Although some of his quests were inspired by petty whims, most of them were undertaken in seek of fulfilling lofty ambitions. Odin was not always the omnipotent God he came to be; he started off as the god of death but the rest of his reign was hard won.

Odin found limitations to his power abhorrent and to take down those barriers he would take all means necessary, ruthless or otherwise. He sought for more wisdom, knowledge and power—often a magical kind.

Sovereignty

As the king of the Æsir gods, Odin had a predilection for society's elite class. He is believed to be the founder of many royal lines and the kings were more or less his shamanistic warriors.

Like many Indo-European society, the Norse society had three social strata over which the gods and goddesses ruled. The upper class included the rulers and sovereignty; the middle class, the warriors; and the lower class, the farmers and fecundity. Odin and Tyr were the rulers of the upper class. There were stark differences between Odin and Tyr. Odin ruled by magic and cunning while Tyr ruled by law and order. Odin carried a rather discreditable imagery, depicted as the malicious, unfathomable one, whereas Tyr was perceived as the virtuous and sober ruler.

Interestingly, Odin was favored by outlaws in exile. These men likened Odin in their disregard for social standards and their strong-will. Egil's Saga (Egill Skallagrimsson) and The Sagga of Grettir the Strong (GrettirÁsmundarson) are prominent examples of his followers. Odin sympathized with this class as he was once condemned to exile for his shamanistic practice of seiðr (which is broadly discussed below).

Those who sought honor, prestige and nobility worshipped Odin, irrespective of their social status.

War

Odin was the god of war; but in contrast to the other noble war gods such as Thor and Tyr, he was a sinister god who incited strife among peaceful people. His concerns lie not in the genesis or the outcome of war but in the brutality of the battles.

As he had a strong bond with the sovereignty he would cherish them with his unending blessings and power. Heroes such as Starkaðr and the Völsungfamily would enjoy his patronage.

He kept a close relationship with the berserkers and other warrior-shamans. Their fighting techniques and pertinent spiritual practices came from Odin and the ecstatic unification with savage, totem animals, often wolves and bears.

Those who fell in the war would be collected by the Valkyries (choosers of the slain). They would then be taken to Odin's Valhalla and feast there and prepare for the final war of Ragnarök.

Wisdom and Magic

He sacrificed his one eye to Mimir for wisdom—he drank from the well of Mimir which was the foundation of wisdom. This explains the eye-patch he always wore. To master the craft of runic magic, he carried out the extreme sacrifice of hanging himself on the Yggdrasil for nine nights and nine days. During this tribulation he accepted no form of nurture from any one of his companions. In the end he was awarded the runes with the magically charged ancient Norse alphabet believed to hold numerous secrets of existence. Odin then vaunted:

"Then I was fertilized and grew wise;

From a word to a word I was led to a word,

From a work to a work I was led to a work."

Shamanism

Odin along with Freya was one of the pantheons that practiced shamanism. The Shaman is of course expected to go through the ritual dying and resurrecting so as to get hold of his/her divine powers. Odin did go through this rigmarole in his earlier venture for the runes. And like any shaman, Odin was accompanied by many spirits; among them were his handmaidens, Valkyries (choosers of the slain), Munin and Hugin, the ravens, and Freki and Geri, the wolves.

This power of Odin's, much like the others, was not acquired effortlessly; in fact, this cost him nine years of exile from Asgard for the shame he had befallen.

The practice of Shamanism is quite difficult to depict. There were different kinds of the practice. Under Odin's patronage were berserkers and other prominent warrior-shamans. It was a socially tolerable practice for Nordic men.

Another form of Nordic Shamanism that was abhorred by society was the pre-Christian Norse Magic ritual of Seidr or Seiðr (pronounced SAY-der). The engagement of a man in seiðr required he assume the role of a women, both sexually and socially. To the Nordic society, this was unacceptable and loathsome. Men who practiced seiðr were gravely ostracized; they were called *ergi* (Old Norse for "unmanly") which in those days was a horrible name to be called. The unmentionable consequences the practice of Seiðr brought notwithstanding,some Norsemen pursued the practice unabashed (this is according to the sagas).

The practice would bestow the practitioner a sort of prophetic insight into the future and allow him/her to alter it by reweaving destiny's web. The practitioner would appear with a distaff in hand and enter a hypnotic state—induced through several methods. He would then make a journey throughout the Nine Worlds and fulfill his desired task.

In depicting the uses of seiðr, archaeologist Neil Price writes:

"There were *seiðr* rituals for divination and clairvoyance; for seeking out the hidden, both in the secrets of the mind and in physical locations; for healing the sick; for bringing good luck; for controlling the weather; for calling game animals and fish. Importantly, it could also be used for the opposite of these things – to curse an individual or an enterprise; to blight the land and make it barren; to induce illness; to tell false futures and thus to set their recipients on a road to disaster; to injure, maim and kill, in domestic disputes and especially in battle"

Odin was not exempt from the consequences of practicing the seiðr. Besides being exiled from Asgard, he was scathed for the feminine traits he adapted and the tasks he carried out during the practice of seiðr. To the pre-Christian Norsemen his practice made him a transgender who was unfitted for a God.

"By his stage-tricks and his assumption of a woman's work he had brought the foulest scandal on the name of the gods" An excerpt from Saxo.

It should be noted that Odin was never chastened by customs or reprehension; nothing stood between him and his ambitions.

Odin's shamanic spirit-journeys were thoroughly documented in the *YnglingaSaga*. And in the **Eddic poem** "Baldur's Dreams", Odin's journey to the underworld with his eight-legged horse Sleipnir is chronicled. The travel was taken in seek of consultancy from a deceased seeress on behalf of Baldur, his son.

Poetry

Odin had to steal the mead of poetry –this was the source from which stemmed the artistry of exquisite speech and persuasiveness—from the giants. That's how he became the god of poetry. He spoke only in poems and bestowed poetic talent to gods, humans and others he deemed worthy of the gift.

Thor

Thor was the eldest son of Jörð, the giantess, and Odin. He was the protector of both Asgard and Midgard. He constantly battled the giants who attempted to bring harm to these realms.

In Norse mythology, this brawny, bearded god had a major presence. In Old Norse he was known as **Þórr**; **Donar,** in Old High German,; and Old English, **Đunor**. Thor was the god of thunderstorm, war and fertility. He would glide through the skies with his goat-drawn chariot (the two goats were Tanngnjóstr and

Tanngrisni). His hammer Mjölnir, his iron glove and his magic belt were his most valued possessions.

Thor's spouse was Sif and his mistress was Járnsaxa; from these relationships he fathered two sons Magni and Modi and a daughter Thurd.

Warrior

Unparalleled in his strength, Thor would dutifully protect the Æsir and their fortress. He was the epitome of a faithful and honorable warrior.

Thor's arch-nemesis was the sea serpent Jormungand who plagued the human race of Midgard. There would often be confrontations between the two eminent figures, but their last was in the final battle of Ragnarök in which the duo ended up annihilating one another.

Consecration

Those in seek of vanity, security, and the hallowing of things, places and events (like weddings) invoked Thor's help. Evidence of this are the relics of runic inscriptions where the people appealed to Thor for the blessing of their desired cause. The first Icelandic settlers invoked the hallowing of Thor before they built their homes and cultivated the land.

Thor's Role in the Society

Archeological finds evidence that Thor's reverence amongst the traditional European society dates back to the Bronze ages. Thor was the principal deity of the middle class—the warriors. But he always had this strong connection with the lower class—the farmers and the fecundity. Notably, in the Viking ages where there was a wave of societal confusion and innovation, Thor's bond with this class was fortified. He became the prominent deity of the commoners in Scandinavia along with the colonies.

The rule of Odin and Thor were very different. Thor's homely qualities were a stark contrast to Odin's gifts of ecstasy, knowledge and magical power. This would often create strife between father and son.

Odin would scorn Thor saying:

"Odin's are the nobles who fall in battle, but Thor's are the thralls."

Throughout the Viking Age (c. 793-1000 CE), however, there was a major demographic shift, and Thor grew more popular than Odin.

Another reason for Thor's popularity in this epoch was the imposition of Christianity on the Scandinavian and colonial communities. The populace tolerated the new religion but when it became clear that Christianity wasn't going to extend the same courtesy, the people chose to even the scores. And when it came to defending the people and their social values, no one paralleled Thor. He was embodied in every form of their disobedience. In defiance of the Christian customs of crucifixes, this rebellious society wore necklaces with the carving of Thor's hammer. There were archeological findings of these hammer pendants in locations where Christianity was most dominant.

Freya

Blessed with beauty unmatched by any Æsir, Freya (or in Old Norse Freyja) was the goddess of love, fertility, and the practice of Seidr. Although she was not at first in the family of Æsir (she was a member of the Vanir tribes of deities) she was later introduced into the family after the Æsir-Vanir war.

Freya was the daughter of Njord and although her mother is unknown, she is believed to be the child of Nerthus.

Her fondness for love, beauty, fertility and the ownership of fine material was quite eminent. She was a free soul.

Freya had a liking for thrills and pleasure and she was probably the most promiscuous goddess. In the Eddic poems, Loki accuses her of sleeping with all the gods—her brother included— and elves. He was probably not wrong.

Sedir or Seiðr (Freya the *Völva)*

This topic has been discussed extensively in the sub-chapter of Odin. Freya was the archetype of a *Völva*—a professional or semi-professional of Seiðr. She was a traveling seeress (a sort of prophetic god) and sorceress who journeyed from one town to the other and one farm to farm carrying out the bespoken acts of Seiðr (magic). In exchange she would be granted temporary housing, food, and other gifts.

Freya was the first one to introduce Seiðr to the gods—as discussed earlier, Odin followed suit.

Loki

Loki (pronounced LOAK-ee) is a very cunning god in Norse mythology. He was the son of the Fárbauti (cruel striker) and Laufey (she could be a giantess, goddess or another being—the literary sources fail to clarify.

In the Edda's and Sagas Loki is depicted as a solitary entity. He is a spineless coward who basks in petty pleasure and self-preservation. Although he can be helpful at times he was a rather unpredictable and devious soul. He was a trickster god.

His craftiness was perhaps most exhibited in his successful con where he convinced the equally sly dwarves to smith different magical objects of the gods—particularly Thor'sMjölnir.

Loki's Offspring

Loki had quite an interesting and rather dreadful progeny. By the giantess Angrboða ("Anguish-Boding") he fathered Hel, Jormungand, the enormous serpent who was the arch-nemesis of Thor and the one who, in the battle of Ragnarök, kills him. He was also the father of Fenrir, the wolf who, during Ragnarök, consumes Odin and bites off the hands of Tyr.

Fenrir is later killed by Odin's son Viðarr.

Loki's engineering of Baldur's death

Although, Loki was tolerated for his many actions against the gods, his orchestration of the death of Baldur put an end to his relationship with the deities.

Frigg, the mother of Baldur learns of her child's dream in which he sees his imminent death. Terrified by this prophesy, she goes around, securing the promise of every creature not to ever harm her son. She manages to get the oath from everyone but the mistletoe who the gods deemed harmless. But Loki knew better. He crafted a sphere made out of the mistletoe and instructed the blind God Hod or Höðr (who was also the brother of Baldur) to shoot it at Baldur. As a result, Baldur dies and is taken Helheim or Hel (the underworld). Hermod, rides there with the eight-legged horse Sleipnir and pleads with goddess Hel to free Baldur and explains how he is loved and missed by all living things.

To this entreaty, Hel proposes an ultimatum: that every creature weeps for the release of Baldur. She said:

"If all things in the world, alive or dead, weep for him, then he will be allowed to return to the Æsir. If anyone speaks against him or refuses to cry, then he will remain with Hel."

Every creature does indeed cry for his return except one: a frost-hearted giantess named Þökk, which was one of Loki's disguises. As a consequence, Baldur is condemned to Helheim until the battle of Ragnarök.

Punishment

For the engineering of Baldur's death and many other crimes, Loki is tied down to three rocks by the entrails of his son with a venomous serpent atop dripping poison on him. Loki's devout wife Sigyn would sit beside him with a bowl in her hands to capture the dripping poison. However, the bowl would seldom fill up and she would leave to pour it out. At this instance the venom would fall on Loki causing him blood-curdling pain. He would squirm in agony and these convulsions would create an earthquake.

In the battle of Ragnarök he attacks Asgard with the giants and helps them carry out the devastating strike.

Frigg

Frigg (pronounced FRIG) was the goddess of atmosphere. She was the supreme leader of the Æsir goddesses. She was the mother of Baldur and the consort of Odin. She is most celebrated for her foreknowledge.

Oddly, for a goddess of her eminent stature, little is said about her in the literary sources and Norse Mythology.

She had so many common traits with Freya. She too belonged to the tribe of Vanir and Æsir deities. Like Freya she was also a *Völva.*

Frigg too was accused of infidelity by Loki—and his accusation had grounds. The *Lokasenna* and the *Ynglinga Saga* relates that during his exile, Odin left his brothers Ville and Vi in command of Asgard. Frigg would sleep with both of them on various occasions until the return of Odin.

Baldur

Baldur or Balder (pronounced BALD-er) was the god of purity and light in Norse mythology. He was the offspring of Frigg and Odin, the father of Forseti and the consort of the goddess Nanna.

All the deities loved and cherished Baldur.

"He's loved by all the gods, goddesses, and beings of a more physical nature. So handsome, gracious, and cheerful is he that he actually gives off light"

--SnorriSturluson. The Prose Edda. Gylfaginning

His death, described thoroughly in the sub-chapter of Loki, was a severe blow to the Æsirs.

Baldur was the one who heralded the coming of the Ragnarök. It was after the momentous battle of Ragnarök he returned to the land of the living. He was then committed to cherishing the souls of the inhabitants of the newborn world.

Hel

Hel is both a goddess and giantess. She is the ruler of Niflheimand Helheim—the underworld where the dead dwelled, otherwise known as Hel. According to the literary works of SnorriSturluson, Poetic Edda, Prose Edda, and Heimskringla, Hel is Loki's daughter. This makes her the sibling of the wolf *Fenrir* and the serpent *Jormungand*.

Hel is vaguely-defined in the literature of Old Norse, but what can be understood from the bits of her mention is that she was greedy and had little concern over the matters of the dead and the living. In the Heimskringla book Ynglinga saga authored bySnorriSturluson, Hel is briefly mentioned (although not by name) at the death of King Dyggvi.

"I doubt not

butDyggvi's corpse

Hel does hold

to whore with him;

for Ulf's sib

a scion of kings

by right should

caress in death:

to love lured

Loki's sister

Yngvi's heir

o'er all Sweden."

Heimdall

Heimdall (pronounced "HAME-doll) was the indefatigable protector of Asgard. He dwells in *Himinbjörg* (Sky Cliffs) which is located at the top of Bifrost—a rainbow bridge leading to Asgard.

Heimdall slept fewer hours than a bird and had phenomenal hearing and eyesight. He can see four hundred miles away both at night and broad day light. So sharp was his hearing abilities, that he was able to hear the growth of grass on the ground and that of wool on sheep.

He would wait vigilantly with his resounding horn Gjallarhorn and warn the other gods when intruders would approach the fortress Asgard.

During Ragnarök, Heimdall sounded his Gjallarhorn, signaling the arrival of the giants. The gods knew they were approaching their doom as they heard this signal. The giants crossed the rainbow bridge and stormed Asgard ruthlessly and killed the gods.

Loki in cahoots with the giants faces Heimdall in the final battle. The world pulverizes and goes under the sea as they slay each other in the fierce fight.

Mimir

Mimir (pronounced "MEE-meer) was the consultant of the gods. He was the wise one. It is quite vague if he was a god or a giant. He lived in Mímisbrunnr (a well). This was the very same well where Odin sacrificed his eye to drink from; this was when he was in seek of wisdom.

Mimir was slain by the Vanir during the Æsir-Vanir war.

Sif

Little is said about Sif in Norse mythology; however, what is certain is that she was the wife of Thor.

In some of the literary sources it is said that she was the mother of the similarly obscure god Ullr, whose father is unknown but is definitely not Thor.

In *"The Creation of Thor's Hammer"* Sif is briefly mentioned although she played no significant role. The tale relates that Loki cuts off her beautiful long hair. Infuriated by his malice, Thor threatens to end his life but Loki convinces him otherwise. He promises Thor that he would find a fairer head for Sif. Thor agrees and Loki sets out for the quest.

Váli

Váli or Vali is the son of the giantess Rindr and Odin. In the Old Norse literature little accounts exist of him. But he had numerous siblings; amongst them were Thor and Baldur. It is believed that *Váli was born to avenge* Höðr who killed Baldur unknowingly—he was cheated by Loki. He grew into full adulthood only a day after his birth and slew Höðr.

He is destined to overcome the Ragnarök. He is mentioned in Baldursdraumar:

"Rindr will bear Váli

in western halls;
that son of Óðinn
will kill when one night old—
he will not wash hand,
nor comb head, before he bears to
the pyre
Baldr's adversary."
– translated by Ursula Dronke's
translation

Vali is also mentioned in Völuspá:

"There formed from that stem,
which was slender-seeming,
a shaft of anguish, perilous:
Hǫðr started shooting.
A brother of Baldr
was born quickly: he started—
Óðinn's son—
slaying, at one night old."

CHAPTER III

The Nine Worlds

The Norse cosmology (Old Norse *NíuHeimar*) consisted of Nine Worlds. It was a place where all beings lived. At the center of the cosmos lied *Yggdrasil* (the world-tree) and it was on the roots and branches of this tree that the worlds existed.

The branches and roots of Yggdrasil were channels to the different worlds such as Nidavellir, Midgard, Svartalfheim, Asgard, Jotunheim, Vanaheim, Alfheim, Niffleheim, and Muspelheim.

There were Ten Worlds initially, but Odin excluded Heven from Yggdrasil after the strife between Heven and Asgard which claimed the life of Aldrif (his infant child).

There are three wells at its base: Hvergelmir (Roaring Kettle), home to the monster Nidhogg; Urdarbrunnr (Well of Fate); and Mimisbrunnr (Mirmir's Well)—this was the source of wisdom and the very same well from which Odin drank from, sacrificing his eye in exchange.

Asgard
Asgard (Old Norse *Ásgarðr)* is the home and fortress of the ÆsirGods and Goddesses. Asgard is located in the sky and is connected to Midgard by the rainbow bridge Bifrost. Each prominent

god has his own palace in Asgard and Odin and his wife, Frigga, are the rulers of Asgard. As depicted by the myths, it is a place bathed in silver and gold. The wonderful rivers, seas, and woodlands are populated by a legion of creatures similar to the ones on Earth: horses, cats and dogs. There were also other creatures alien to Earth: various kinds of sea serpents and dragons.

Valhalla (in Old Norse *Valhöll*) is one other very special section located in Asgard. The doors of Valhalla are very spacious that it even permits 800 warriors to walk side by side. Valhalla was surrounded by walls of spear shafts and roofed by golden shields. It is a heaven in which half the dead Viking warriors would come for their afterlife. Freya would take the other half of the deceased Vikings. Each Viking sent to Valhalla would wake up every morning and fight on Asgard's large tracts of land. These were the dress-rehearsals for the final war, Ragnarök. The warriors might suffer severe casualties during these fights but they would be instantly restored and healed.

Vanaheim

Positioned around Yggdrasil, the world-tree, Vanaheim (Old Norse *Vanaheimr)* is a component of the Nine Worlds. The name "heim" means home. The Vanir deities lived there; they were unparalled in their mastery of magic, sorcery and prophecy. Frigga's talent over sorcery is unmatched to no other that she was the one who taught the secrets of magic to Odin.

Following the momentous battle of the Vanir and the Æsir, three of the Vanir migrated to Asgard —Njord and his offspring Freyr and Freya.

Vanaheim is a majestic world, encircled with pure, vast bodies of water and wooded areas, which were inhabited by spirits and animals.

Alfheim

Alfheim (Old Norse *Álfheimr)* is the homeland of the light elves. It is situated next to Asgard. The elves are depicted as being luminous and "more beautiful than the sun." They are regarded as the "guardian angels." Freyr, the Vanir god, is believed to be Alfheim's leader.

The relation of the light elves with humans is at times dubious. Often, elves bring about illnesses to humans, but they also posses the magical ability to cure these ailments. Their motivation to cure is especially heightened if they are presented with a certain kind of sacrifice. The interbreeding of elves and humans is possible and they can create half-elfin, half-human children, who have the appearance of human beings but with amazing magical powers.

Midgard

Midgard (*Miðgarðr* in Old Norse) is the home of mankind and part the Nine Worlds in Norse Mythology. Midgard is also known as "middle earth". It is situated in the core of a world that's beneath Asgard. What connects Asgard and Midgard is the world called Bifrost the Rainbow Bridge, which is guarded by Heimdallr. From the Nine World, Midgard happens to be the only one situated in the visible world. The others are primarily invisible worlds but there are moments where interception with the visible worlds is possible. It is situated halfway between Niflheim on the north, the land of ice, and Muspelheim to the south, the region of fire.

Midgard is encircled with a massive ocean that no one has ever been able to pass. The ocean is occupied by Jörmungandr (Miðgarðsormr), the great sea serpent, who is so massive that he surrounds the whole world, grasping his own tail.

In North Mythology, the middle earth (the land of humanity), is made from the body of the first created being, the giant Aurgelmir (Ymir) after the gods slew him. Aurgelmir's body became the land; his blood turned into oceans; his teeth, the cliffs; his bones became mountains; his hairs, the trees; and his brains (scattered all over the earth), the clouds. With his eyebrows he erected a hedge around Midgard to safeguard it and all its inhabitants from the intrusion of the giants.

Jotunheim

Jotunheim (Old Norse *Jötunheimr)* is the home of the jotuns (giants). They are the arch-nemesis of the Æsir.

Jotunheim is composed of dense forests, rocks and wilderness. The giants and the Æsirwere engaged in constant battles. Jotunheim is where Loki, the son of the Giants, Farbauti and, was born. Odin adopted Loki after he had slaughtered his father, Laufey.

Jotunheim is situated amidst the Norse universe. A river that never freezes divides it from Asgard. It is in a frosty area found on the farthest coast of the ocean. Mirmir's Well of Wisdom is to be found in Jotunheim, under the second root of the Yggdrasil "the world-tree". Utgarðar is the capital of Jotunheim, functioning as a stronghold of the giants.

Svartalfheim

Svartalfheim (Old Norse *Svartálfaheim*) is a realm in the Nine Worlds that is inhabited by the dwarves, who are frequently called in the Old Norse literature as "dark elves" (Old Norse *svartálfar*). Svartalfheim is at the core of the nine realms, situated on the exact plane as Midgard and Jotunheim.

The realm is greatly wooded with Dark Elf towns, villages and castles all over the green rolling landscape. They have been shown to dwell both in castles above ground and in large caverns underground. The Dark Elves possessed their own portal that permits them to access the other Nine Worlds.

Often, the Dark Elves were treated unfavorably by the inhabitants of the nine realms owing to their appearance. They were,therefore, hostile towards outsiders. The black elves are considered as pesky creatures that are nothing but trouble. Several Norsemen and Norsewomen assumed that the dark elves were highly responsible for nightmares. They were often called mare. This mare would murmur daunting dreams to trouble a person while sitting on their chest. It is also said that a mare could haunt animals too, specifically horses.

Nildavellir

Nildavellir (*Niðavellir* in Old Norse) is the homeland of the diminutive and elusive tribe of the humanoid known as the dwarves (Dvergr). They dwelled in caves, under the rocks and underground. The dwarves are skilled craftspeople. The Æsir deities have received several powerful gifts such as the magical ring Draupnir, Gungnir, Odin's spear and Thor's hammer. Nidavellir's ruler was Hreidmar. (Nidavellir is also known as the "Dark fields''.)

Niflheim

Niflheim (*Niflheimr* in Old Norse) is one of the realms in the Nine Worlds. Legends describe Niflheim as being an awfully cold and icy landscape of infinite night. Nilfheim is the hostile world of the dead who were remorselessly evil and malicious in their living days. The souls confined there were subjected to continual hardships and torture. They were also condemned to live under the reign of Hel, the goddess of death.

Niflheim was initially inhabited by Ymir and later, by the giants whom he seeded during the primitive years of the Nine Worlds. Ymir came to live when fire from Muspelheim and ice from Niflheim collided at the core of Ginnungagap, an abyss formerly responsible for separating them.

Helheim

(Old Norse *Helheimr "the world of the goddess Hel"*) is part of the Nine Worlds. Also known as "Hel", Helheim is the underworld where the souls of the gods and mortals dwelled in, under the sovereignty of Hel, the goddess of death. Helheim is located underground and it's described to be the kingdom of lifelessness and sheer frost.

Though the two realms, Niflheim and Helheim, are two separate spheres, they are often deemed to be "one" of the Nine Worlds as they are the afterlife realms governed by the goddess Hel.

Muspelheim

Muspelheim (Old Norse *Múspellsheimr*) is one of the Nine Worlds in Asgardian cosmology which is the dwelling of the fire giants and fire demons. Muspelheim is a realm of fire riddled with lava, flames, spars and soot. It is governed by the fire giant Surt, a sworn enemy of the Æsir. It was the homeland of Warlock's Eye.

Chapters IV

Heroes and Legends

The Norsemen had quite a lot of heroes and legends, ones that were idolized and worshiped throughout the whole of Scandinavia. And it was because of these extraordinary figures that Norse history has come to be this unceasing and timelessly captivating entity in human recordings.

And amongst the most renowned heroes and legends in Norse Mythology are Ragnar Lodbrok, Björn Ironside, Beowulf, Sigmund, and Sigurd.

Ragnar Lodbrok

Ragnar Lodbrok or **'Reginherus'**, in Old Norse, was a Norse ruler and a hero who's best known for his execution of a successful raid in France. Ragnar's conquering and raiding days were long and very colorful. But what engraved his name in the history books and what elevated him to that platform of widespread adulation was his raid in France, in 845 A.D. This event in France didn't just steep Ragnar in great riches; it was also what marked the beginning of his life as a hero and later on, ruler of the Norse.

According to the legends, prior to the raid, Ragnar was living peacefully in Tuhot, France, on a land given to him by King Charles the Bald. But then the powers-that-be decided to confiscate that land and rid him of ownership.

Swamped with rage and driven by revenge, Ragnar then assembled his army, which is said to be of about 5000 men, and with a fleet of over 100 long-ships, he entered France. The French army did whatever was possible to stop the invasion of Ragnar's army, but it proved to be impossible. Ragnar was too angry and too powerful to defeat.

And so at the end, when all alternatives were bleak, Charles the Bald decided to seek out a resolution and offered Ragnar 2,570 kilograms of silver and gold to withdraw. Ragnar accepted the offer, and the raid was finally brought to an end.

Ragnar lived a life of colorful adventures. According to the sagas, Ragnar was married three times and had many children, some of whom were Halfdan Ragnarsson, Sigurd Snake-in-the-Eye, Björn Ironside, Ubba and Ivar the Boneless,.

His end however was rather gloomy. Legend has it that Ragnar was imprisoned by the King of Northumbria, Ælla, and later sentenced to death by the unforgiving sting of venomous snakes. Soon after, his sons, mainly Halfdan Ragnarsson, Ubba and Ivar the Boneless, avenged his death by assembling the Great Heathen Army and raiding England.

Björn Ironside

Björn Ironside was the son of the legendary hero Ragnar Lodbrok. He was a powerful Norse chieftain and a naval commander, whose crafty entrance in Rome earned him an eternal spot in Norse history. Björn is also known to be the first ruler of the Munsö dynasty.

Björn's career as a conqueror and a hero began when he first decided to follow in his father's footsteps and went off to raid northern France with his brother Hastein. The invasion was successful but Björn wanted more. And when he heard of Rome, a city of great riches, he was dogged to forge ahead to the Mediterranean and make a history of his own by invading it.

Upon arrival, Björn and his army were faced with a great challenge – the great City Wall proved to be impenetrable. But then he came up with a plan that granted him and his army easy entrance.

He sent the Bishop of Luna a message which said that he had died and that his final wish was a burial spot in the ground of the Holy Christian church. The Bishop, seeing no harm in the request, permitted the entrance of Bjorn's body along with a small honor guard.

Soon after the coffin entered the church, Björn leaped out and while everyone stood shocked and stock-still, he and his honor guard rushed towards the town gates and allowed his army to enter.

Rome was viciously raided and Björn was certainly known for it.

Invigorated by this victory, Björn then went on to raid Sicily and North Africa. But on his return to the Straits of Gibraltar, he was confronted by the Saracen navy at Al-Andalus. Björn's fleet was then attacked by the Greek fire, which resulted in the loss of 40 ships and hundreds of men.

However, Björn did manage to escape the attack and return home with a great amount of fortune.

Soon after his father's death Björn inherited the Kingdom of Sweden. He founded the House of Munsö, a dynasty that ruled both Sweden and Denmark for several generations. House of Munsö is known as the Old Dynasty in Sweden. It is believed to have the name Munsö came from where Björn was buried – the island of Munsö.

Beowulf

Beowulf is a Norse hero, a legendary warrior whose extraordinary skills and brave adventures were celebrated and chronicled tellingly in the epic poem 'Beowulf'.

According to this poem, which happens to be amongst the few surviving relics of the English literature, Beowulf was the son of Ecgtheow, a Swedish warrior, and Hreð, daughter of the Geatish king.

Beowulf was known throughout the Norse land for his courage and strength in battlefields, but what climaxed his name were the daring adventures he embarked upon. And it all began when he heard of the brutal attacks of a monstrous being named Grendel, in the neighboring kingdoms.

Grendel terrorized and slaughtered many inhabitants in Denmark, so much so that even their king, Hroðgar, was left in jitters.

Beowulf, disturbed by this unease, prepared his ship and sailed to Denmark with fourteen warriors he single handedly selected. The king, having heard so much about Beowulf's bravery, was delighted to hear of his coming, and so he prepared a warm welcome for the Geat warriors.

At night Grendel went about his usual attacks on the men who were sleeping and ended up killing and eating some of the warriors. Beowulf, driven by rage, charged at Grendel and tore off his arm using only hands. The beast then fled to his cave and died there. The people celebrated Grendel's death, but the battle was far from over.

On the following night, Grendel's mother entered the castle to avenge her son's death. She attacked the warriors and even killed one of the kings most trusted advisors. Beowulf was unable to rescue them from the beast's fury, but he soon followed her in to the cave and slew her with an enchanted sword.

The hero then returned back to Geatland, where he fought alongside king Higlac in a raid against the Franks. Higlac died in this battle while Beowulf returned to the kingdom unscathed. Enthused by his bravery the queen, Hygd, offered him the throne. However, Beowulf refused to take the seat away from the rightful heir, prince Heardred.

But the ruling days of the young prince was cut short. When the Swedish prince, Eadgils, was ousted by his uncle Onela, the Geats decided to invade Sweden and restore the throne back to its rightful keeper. In this battle, Heardred was killed and Onela was slain. The event in which Onela was killed has been broadly illustrated in 'The Battle of the Ice of Lake Vähern' by SnorriSturluson.

Here is an excerpt:

"Onela rode Raven, as they rode to the ice, but a second one, a grey one, hastened, wounded by spears, eastwards under Eadgils...... In this fight Onela died and a great many of his people. Then king Eadgils took from him his helmet battle-boar and his horse Raven."

Beowulf then became the ruler of the Geats, and stayed as such until his time of death, which was 51 years later. Beowulf didn't die sick or old; he succumbed from a wound inflicted on him by the dragon he had slain. He surly lived and died as a hero.

Sigmund

Sigmund was a hero most commonly known for being the only one who was able to pull out the enchanted sword from the ever so mighty Branstock tree.

Sigmund had nine brothers and a twin sister named Signy. His parents were Völsung and Hljod. Sigmund's adventures began when he drew the sword out of the flesh of the Branstock tree. This sword was said to have been placed by Odin himself and that it would enable its bearer to win all wars with it.

Hearing of this, Siggeir, Signy's husband, asked for Sigmund to sell him the sword. But it didn't take much for the Norse hero to decline the offer. Then Siggeir, stewing in rage for begin refused, did whatever was possible to destroy Völsung and his family. And with the help of his shape-shifting mother, Siggeirmanaged to kill Völsung and his nine sons, but not Sigmund— his twin sister Signy helped him escape.

To avenge their family's death Sigmund and Signy then became an alliance. Sigmund dwelled in the woods as Signy sent him whatever he needed from the palace. But they were too small of a force to defeat Siggeir and his army. So she disguised herself as a völva and managed to be with Sigmund and conceive a child named Singjötli.

With Singjötli by his side, Sigmund was then able to avenge his family's death. They torched the palace and managed to kill Siggeir and everyone in it, except for Signy.

Sigmund then returned to his homeland with Singjötli and became king. He got married to Borghild and had two children with her, Helgi and Hamund. But the marriage didn't last for long. Borghild ended up poisoning Singjötli. According to the legends, she either killed him out of vengeance for killing her brother, or out of sheer hatred.

Nevertheless, after banishing Borghild for murdering his son, Sigmund fell in love and got married again to the daughter of King Eylimi, Hjordis.

Peace, however, never seems to settle for Sigmund. Hjordis had another suitor, King Lyngi. And when she got married to Sigmund, he grew envious and vengeful. Eventually, Lyngi waged war against Sigmund and his father in-law Eylimi.

In this battle Eylimi was killed and Odin in disguise of an old beggar fought Sigmund and shattered the sword to pieces, which left him vulnerable to the attacks of his enemy. Sigmund was severely wounded and on his death bed, he asked his pregnant wife, Hjordis, to collect the shattered sword and to give it to their son when he grows up.

Their son was the dragon slaying warrior, Sigurd.

Sigurd

Sigurd, the legendary dragon slaying warrior, was the son of Sigmund and Hjordis.

After the death of Sigmund, Hjordis ran away to Denmark and got married King Alf. Alf raised Sigurd as though he was his own son, and once he grew up he went off to stay with his tutor Regin, who happened to be Hreidmar's son and the brother of Fafnir and Ótr.

On the day of his leave his mother gave him the fragments of his father's magical sword and his step father gave him the permission to choose a horse he desired, and he chose Grani, the grey horse— a decision influenced by a one eyed old man, who was Odin in disguise.

Regin wanted to get his hands on his brother's treasures, and he knew that Sigurd would be able to get him just that. So he brain washed the boy into thinking that wealth and power were the only entities in life worth living for. Then he told him about Otter's Gold, how Loki gave this enormous gold to the family as acompensation for killing Ótr, and how Fafnir killed their father, Hreidmar, and took all the treasure with him.

Sigurd then agreed to kill Fafnir and avenge him and his father. But the Andvari's ring and gold had already turned Fafnir into a dragon. And when Sigurd learned of this transformation, he asked Regin to make him a strong sword. Every sword that Regin made was fragile and every test strike kept on shattering it. But then Sigurd took out the fragments of his father's sword and asked him to mend it. The sword was mended and it proved to be as strong as it once was.

Before facing the dragon, however, Sigurd wanted to avenge his father's death. And so he assembled his army and headed for King Lyngi. And he did so with great success.

Sigurd then went toGnitaheath or 'Glittering Heath' where Fafnir dwelt. He prepared a trap and when it was least expected, Sigurd killed the dragon by stabbing it in the back.

Following the counsel of this old man, Sigurd then drank Fafnir's blood. Regin had asked him to give him the dragon's heart, and Sigurd agreed but still had a taste of it. The blood gave him the ability to hear and talk to birds and the heart gave him wisdom, strength and courage.

The birds then told him that Regin would betray him and take all the treasure away once he eats the dragon's heart. And so Sigurd beheaded Regin on the spot.

Sigurd then fell in love with the daughter of Budli, Brynhild (or Burnhild). He found her sleeping at the mountaintop of Hindfell surrounded by a ring of fire — she was being punished by Odin for disobedience. He woke her up from her sleep and they fell in love.

Despite the breathtaking beginning of their love affair though, magic and the curse of the Andvari's ring and gold destined them to a terrible end.

CHAPTER V

Mythological Creatures

The Gods, the heroes, the legends and the nine realms are obviously elements that have made out the enchanting colors of Norse Mythology. But the role of the divine creatures has also proved to be of paramount importance. Without these odd yet interesting beings, Norse Mythology would have certainly been incomplete.

Valkyries

Valkyries or 'valkyrja' in Old Norse basically means 'Choosers of the fallen' or 'Choosers of the slain'. The Valkyries were female spirits, twelve to be specific, and they were Odin's handmaidens.

The Valkyries were creatures who would ride their horses to the battle fields and escort the souls of dead warriors to the Valhalla. Odin would then have his selected heroes— who have proved themselves to be the bravest, the strongest and the most courageous of their comrades—fight with him in the Ragnarök.

According to various sagas, the Valkyries were elegant beings. They were creatures that opened the portal through which brave warriors could enter the Valhalla, so they were never perceived as an ominous entity. But their deeds weren't always as chaste and godly. The Valkyries weren't just the kinds to select the souls of heroes that have already been dead; they were also the kinds to use magic and get their selected warriors killed in battle fields.

The gloomy aspect of the Valkyries is illustrated in the poem in the Njal's Saga, where the twelve Valkyries crafted the destiny of warriors in the Battle of Clontarf.

Norns

The Norns, in Norse mythology, were the three goddesses of destiny. Their names were Urd or Urðr, which means 'what once was'; Verdandi or Verðandi, meaning 'What is coming into being'; and Skuld or Skula, meaning 'What shall be'.

The Norns were three divine beings that had the greatest amount of influence over the course of destiny. No other creature in Norse mythology had as much power and wisdom as they did. They were simply unmatched.

They lived in the Well of Urd under the shade of the great ash tree or World-tree, Yggdrasil, the tree that carries the Nine Worlds in its roots and branches and stands at the center of the universe.

The Norns would structure fate by engraving runes onto the trunk of the World-tree or weaving it like a tapestry.

But the destiny the Norns have carved is the kind that permits the individual to influence its course to a certain extent.

Jotuns

The Jotuns were giants that possessed the strength and power that no other creature had. They were magical beings that lived in the wilderness of Jotunheim.

The first jotun or giant was Ymir, from whose armpit grew the race of giants. In Norse mythology they were creatures considered to be chaotic. In most sagas they are referred to as spirits of the night, winter, and death.

The giants were a great challenge to Aesir's, as they would often pose as an unforgiving enemy of his.

Amongst the most known giants are Hel, the daughter of Loki and Angrboda and ruler of the underworld; Fenrir, the wolf that devoured Odin during Ragnarök; Aegir and Ran, rulers of the sea; Nidhogg, the snake that nibbled at the roots of the Yggdrasil; Jormungand, the sea serpent and so forth.

Dwarfs

In Norse mythology, Dwarfs or Dvergr, in Old Norse, doesn't quite necessarily mean 'small people'. They are illustrated as divine creatures that are unmatched in their craftsmanship.

The dwarfs are known and praised for their incredible set of skills. They have crafted innumerable things that have proved to be indispensable in Norse mythology: the Mjöllnir (Thor's hammer);

Odin's spear (the Gungnir); Freyr's ship (the Skiðblaðnir); the chain Gleinir that ensnared the wolf Fenrir are but a few.

These creatures were also known to be wise and powerful. They lived underground in a place called Svartalfheim. And legend has it that they turn to stone when exposed to the sun.

According to the sagas, the dwarfs were also creatures that sustain the expanse of the horizon. As it was noted, there were four dwarves that held the four corners of the sky; Austri (the East), Vestri (the West), Suðri (the South), and Norðri (the North).

Light Elves and Dark Elves

In Norse mythology, elves are described as godly creatures that are bright and more beautiful than even the sun itself.

The elves lived in Alfheim, a land ruled by the Vanir god Freyr. And there are two different kinds of elves in Norse Mythology; the light elves and the dark elves.

The light elves are described to be the one of the world's most attractive beings. And according to various sagas they had a rather intimate association with mortal humans.

They were the gods of fertility and nature, and were often regarded as guardian angels. But these elves had great magical powers and they would sometimes use it to cause pain and anguish to humans, which they would willingly reverse if they are presented with certain kinds of sacrifices.

The dark elves, on the other hand were hideous beings that bring nothing but trouble to humans. They are believed to be the ones who cause nightmares and so they were often referred to as mares.

Dark elves live underground, and much like dwarfs, exposure to sun would turn them in to stones.

Ten Little Known Facts about Norse Mythology

There are always those little hidden facts that have not yet been revealed to us. Well, below is a collection of ten little known facts about the Norse Mythology, enjoy!

Odin has two ravens which sit on his shoulders. These are Muninn (memory) and Huginn (thought). The two ravens are sent by Odin around the world to bring back information of what they saw and heard. Hence, the reason why he is called Rafnugod (raven god).

Another factoid from Norse Mythology involves a cow. Initially, it was only the worlds of Niflheim (ice) and Muspelheim (fire) which existed. When the tepid air of Muspelheim collided with that of the extreme frost of Niflheim, Audumbla, the cow, and Ymir, the giant, came to life. A woman and a man emerged from the sweat of Ymir's armpits while he was asleep. Audumbla licked Búri (the first of the Æsir tribe) out of a briny lump of ice while he suckled Ymir.

The famous son of Odin, Thor, was a red head! He is depicted with a red hair and beard.

In Norse Mythology, Thor's affection for Earth emanates from his mother's influence. Thor is the child of Odin and the feminine embodiment of Earth, known as Gaea in other mythologies and as Jörð in Norse mythology (her other names include Hlóðyn and Fjörgyn). At first, the real identity of his mother was not revealed to Thor, and he was made to believe that he was the child of Odin and Frigga.

The seven days of the week are associated with the Norse deities:

Sunday: in association with the deity Balder. labeled after the earthly body which is also connected with the day: the Sun ("Sun Day").

Monday: related with the deity Frigga. Named after the planetary body also connected with the day: the Moon ("Moon Day").

Tuesday: connected with the god Tyr. The day is named after Tyr's Old English name: Tiu ("Tiu's Day").

Wednesday: in relation with the mighty god Odin. The day was named after his Germanic name Wodan ("Wodan's Day").

Thursday: in connection with Thor, the Norse god, the day was labeled after him ("Thor's Day").

Friday: connected with the deity Freya, the day was named after her ("Freya's Day). There are some sources which claim that the name of this day is in fact related to Frigga and not Freya.

Saturday: related with the cosmic personifications or deities who are known as the Norns. Named after the planetary body also related with the day: Saturn ("Saturn's Day").

Norse mythology predates Christianity, so several of the Norse pagan symbols and legends have been merged, morphed or co-opt throughout the years. Did you know that Santa Claus is an amalgamation of Odin and the Christian legend of Saint Nick? Well, children used to leave their shoes, packed with carrots or other edibles next to the chimney for Sleipnir to consume. In exchange, Odin would leave gifts or candy.

Several tales state that Odin traveled on earth. These travels consisted of his "test" of people's behavior, to witness how courteous and friendly they were. If they were in any way hostile or rude, he would punish them.

The Norse god Odin didn't have to eat food, according to legends. For him, wine is both food and drink. The food served on the table is given to the two wolves, Geri and Freki.

According to Norse Mythology, Thor and the other gods of Asgard became immortals by consuming the magical Golden Apples of Idunn. They grow in Asgard and only the deity Idunn can harvest them.

Loki a Mother? Indeed Loki was a mother too; he was a rebellious god who, let's just say, showed no respect to customs and even the laws of nature. He was a shape-shifter who would often appear as a female horse, fish, fly, seal and probably Þökk, an old woman. According to the chronicles of the tale "The Fortification of Asgard", he transforms into a female horse to seduce the stallion Svaðilfari. From this relationship, Loki bears the eight legged serpent Sleipnir; this is the same shamanic horse of Odin.

EGYPTIAN MYTHOLOGY

Of the many nations in this world, it's quite apparent that ancient Egypt has a lot of stories to tell. And there is certainly an ample of interesting elements in the history of this great nation, but what gives a better insight of ancient Egypt and her incredibly imaginative inhabitants happens to be the myths.

The epicenter of the ancient Egyptian culture, Egyptian Mythology consisted of enthralling gods to whom sacrifices and rituals were consecrated. Isis, Osiris, Ra, Horus are but a few. Egyptians were able to export their phenomenal religion and culture through their far reaching trade links.

This eBook contains the many features of the mythology which include the deities, the pharaohs, rites and sacrifices and the mysterious "Book of the Dead". It gives a great insight into the prehistoric Egyptian society.

Near the end of the book there is a bonus chapter full of interesting and fun facts that you would be surprised to learn.

CHAPTER I

Egyptian Mythology

Egyptian Mythology is the accumulation of myths derived from ancient Egypt from at least c. 4000 BCE to 30 CE. The end was marked with the death Cleopatra VII, the last of the Ptolemaic sovereign of Egypt.

Often, in Egyptian writing and art, myths occur— particularly in short stories and in religious materials such as ritual text, hymns, funerary texts and temple decoration. Full accounts of the myth from these sources are rare; they are habitually described in brief fragments.

The Egyptian religion and belief were spread beyond the domain of Egypt through trade, notably after 130 BCE when the Silk Road opened. This made Alexandria the epicenter of commerce. For other cultures, the imperative aspect of Egyptian Mythology was the eternal life after death concept, the reincarnation and benevolent deities. Both Greek philosophers Plato and Pythagoras are believed to be inspired by the belief of Egyptians in reincarnation. What's more, religious cultures from Egypt were largely adopted by the Romans as they did from other civilization.

Natural surroundings influenced the Egyptian myth. Annually, the Nile flooded the land to renew the soil's richness and promote the prosperity of farming that was essential to the civilization of Egypt.

Daily, the sun rose and set to bless the land with light and to watch over the activities of humanity. Thus, in the view of Egyptians, water and the sun were considered the emblem of life. They also viewed time as a chain of natural cycles. Low and high floods threatened the order of this cycle; they caused damage to the cultivation and buildings and brought about famine. The generous Nile valley was encircled by a severe desert that was inhabited by peoples who the Egyptians believed were savage foes who disrupted the order. As a result, they believed their area of habitation was one of stability, secluded from the rest.

To the Egyptians, humanity's existence was believed to be only a tiny part in the journey of eternity. The deities and supernatural agents coordinated and ruled over the course of this voyage.

According to the historian Bunson:

"Heh, called Huh in some eras, was one of the original gods of the Ogdoad [the eight deities worshipped during the Old Kingdom, 2575-2134 BCE] at Hermopolis and represented eternity — the goal and destiny of all human life in Egyptian religious beliefs, a stage of existence in which mortals could attain everlasting bliss (86)."

The existence of someone on this earth was a part of the eternal journey; it was also an introduction to something bigger. The concept of the afterlife for Egyptians was a mirror-world of one's life on earth— particularly, one's life in Egypt. If one desired to enjoy the rest of his/her eternal journey, he was obliged to live that life correctly.

The Creation of the World

The creation of the universe and the world out of whirling chaos and obscurity was where the journey commenced. There was once nothing but infinite dark water devoid of form or purpose. From this bedlam surfaced Ben-Ben (the primeval hill); atop of this hill lived Atum (sometimes, Ptah). Atum observed the emptiness and realized his loneliness. He bred with his shadow to produce two offspring: Tefnut (goddess of moisture, whom Atum vomited out) and Shu (god of air, whom Atum spat out). The principles of order were issued by Tefnut and the principles of life were given by Shu.

After they were born, the siblings set out to create the world, leaving their father on the Ben-Ben. After a while, Atum was overwhelmed by anxiety for his children took long to return. He took out his one eye and sent it to look for them. Much to his relief, Shu and Tefnut returned after some time with his one eye; Atum, grateful for his children's return shed tears of happiness. His tears rained atop the dark and fertile soil of Ben-Ben, thereby producing women and men.

These early beings had no place to dwell, however. Tefnut and Shu, thus, mated and bore the goddess Nut (the Sky) and the god Geb (the earth). The siblings, Geb and Nut, became lovers, inseparable from one another. Unable to brook their unacceptable behavior, Atum took Nut into the heavens, far away from Geb. Both lovers had clear views of one another; however, they were unable to touch. Already impregnated by Geb, Nut gave birth to Set, Osiris, Isis and Nephthys— the prominent Egyptian gods. Osiris was often considered a sensible and thoughtful god which was probably why Atum gave him rule over the world.

Sources

Enjoyable tales and solemn hymns constitute the sources of Egyptian mythology. Illiteracy amongst Egyptians of the time was prevalent so it was mostly the tradition of storytelling that spread the myths. It is suggested by some that this tradition of storytelling explains why little detail of the myths exist—every Egyptian knew about the myths. Evidence showing the survival of this oral tradition is precious little and it is pictorial and written sources that furnish the modern knowledge of Egyptian myths. Only few of these sources managed to survive to current times as many of the writings have been lost.

CHAPTER II

Gods and Goddesses

The gods held great leverage over the daily lives of the ancient Egyptian society. They were the creators of the cosmos and the ones that set order. The gods and goddesses had a cult of their own; rituals as well as sacrifices were held for them.

Isis

Isis (Egyptian Aset or Eset) was the eldest daughter of Geb and Nut. She had four siblings, Osiris, Seth, Nephthys and Haroeris. She was both the sibling and wife of Osiris from whom she bore Horus. Her other offspring were Bastet and probably Ammit.

She was depicted as a beautiful women dressed in sheath and a headdress that either had a solar disc in between a cow's horn or the hieroglyphic sign of the throne. She would also be depicted as a scorpion, cow or a bird. Her symbols were a sparrow, vulture, sycamore tree, cobra and a small hawk.

Isis was unmatched with her magical powers—not even Osiris or Ra could match her skills; she was the goddess of magic but her prowess was indeed diverse. Isis was the goddess of protection, the patron of nature, the dead, children, the noble and the commoners. She was loved and worshiped by all social strata. She had a very close link with the kings and kingship. She answered to the entreaty of the slaves, artisans, sinners, the downtrodden, the aristocrats and the maidens.

As a bereaved soul, she was associated with funeral rituals; as a sorceress, she cured the ill and brought the dead back to life; and as the ideal mother, she was an exemplar of all Egyptian women.

Initially an obscure goddess without temples consecrated to her, she grew famous during the advance of the dynastic age. She became one of the chief deities of ancient Egypt. The cult of Isis spanned across dominions as far distant as the Greco-Roman world, the Roman Empire and Afghanistan.

Isis was the archetype of an ideal wife and mother who was a stout supporter of her husband Osiris. Egyptian women aspired to become the perfect mother and wife she was; she taught them how to weave, brew bear and bake. She was a woman who remained in the background when all was well but would intervene either with her sorcery or sharp wit when it came to protecting her family during precarious times.

The Story of Isis and Osiris

The chronicles of Isis and Osiris is largely depicted in Plutarch's Greek depiction *"De IsideetOsiride"* (written in the 1st century CE).

According to this literary source, Seth, who was envious of the god of Egypt Osiris, contrived a plan to kill him. He held a banquet and, before his guests, displayed an embellished wooden chest. He asked each of them to fit in it and said that he would reward it to the one who did. The box was custom made for Osiris since Seth had measured him in his sleep. When it came to Osiris's turn, he fit in the chest perfectly. Seth then closed the led on him and thrust the box into the river Nile which was to drift him as far away as possible. He then was crowned the pharaoh of Egypt.

Isis wept plentifully over her husband's death. Her tears, it was believed, would induce the flood of the Nile River.

The mourning widow Isis set out to seek his corpse and found it at Byblos by a tree. She brought back the body to Egypt. Seth had learnt of this so he scavenged for the chest. Once he found it, he hacked Osiris' body into pieces (according to some accounts, fourteen peaces) and scattered his corpse all over Egypt.

The dogged Isis was undeterred by the challenge. With the help of her sister Nephthys, she transformed into a bird and managed to collect each part of the corpse of Osiris. All but one: his genitals. Unfortunately, a fish had feasted on that organ and Isis could not recover it. Nonetheless, she was able to replace it with a golden phallus. She was also able to use her magical prowess to stitch up his body with bandages; he was transformed into a mummy neither dead nor alive. With the help of Thoth's magic she was able to bore him a son, Horus after nine months. Osiris then became the ruler of the dead after being condemned to the underworld.

Osiris' demise and reincarnation was revived annually through rituals.

Isis and Her Son Horus

At Khemmis, Isis bore Horus. She fled with her newborn in order to escape the rage of Seth. Horus was endangered by many perils. At one point he was bitten by a poisonous scorpion and Isis had to use her magical skills to heal him. She protected him until he reached the able age to seek vengeance on his father's murderer and claim his throne.

It was for the role she played in guarding her son that she earned the title "goddess of protection".

The Inspiration of Isis on Christianity

The portraits of Isis suckling her newborn Horus served as an inspiration to many Christian paintings of the Virgin Mary with her baby Jesus Christ.

Horus

Horus (Egyptian, Hor, Har, Her, or Heru) was the Egyptian deity of kingship and sun. He was also depicted as the god of War, hunting, Upper Egypt, light, and protection.

Horus was the posthumous son of Osiris and Isis. Serket (Haroeris) and Hathor were believed to be his consorts.

Depicted as a falcon, Horus had a right eye that was deified as the sun (or morning sun) which symbolized power and epitome (Horus was the archetype of a king and the reigning ruler was often thought to be Horus' manifestation). His right eye was the moon (or evening star), symbolizing the power of healing. This was why he was the god of the sky.

The Battle of Horus with Seth

After his birth Horus was pursued relentlessly by the murderer of his father Seth. His mother Isis worked indefatigably to keep him out of harm's way. Once he reached an able age he set out to avenge the murderer of his father and to lay claim to the throne.

The two had unending battles from the 1ˢᵗ dynasty (c. 2925–2775 BCE) onward. Their feud perpetuated for almost a century and was concluded by the triumph of Horus and the merging of Upper and Lower Egypt. Seth was seen as the god of Lower Egypt, and Horus, the god of Upper Egypt. Horus emerged as a victor not because of a triumph in the battles but because of his acquisition of the most votes from the other gods. He came to be known as **Harsiesis, Heru-ur** or **Har-Wer**– translated as **Horus the Great** or **Horus the Elder**. He became the new King of Egypt.

Both warring parties were injured severely. Seth lost his testicles; this explains why the desert he embodies is barren; Seth was the deity that ruled over the desert. Horus, on the other hand, lost his left eye (the moon). It was restored through the magical prowess of Thoth. The eye that was restored was known as "the wedjat eye"; it became a powerful amulet.

Osiris

Osiris (otherwise known as **Usir, Asiri, Ausir** or **Ausar)** was the child of Geb and Nut. He was the ruler of the afterlife, the dead and the underworld. Initially, however, he was the god of the earth. He was the husband of Isis and from her he bore Horus posthumously. Anubis is also believed to his child.

In his depictions, Osiris is a mummy with his hands crossed over his chest. In one hand he held a flail and in the other he had a crook. He wore the after-crown which consisted of two ostrich feathers—the crown resembled that of Upper Egypt.

A yearly ritual to commemorate his death and rebirth would be held. In these festivals processions, sacrifices and nocturnal rites would be held. He was not only believed to be the god that ruled over the dead but also a god with the power to bestow life from the underworld (the afterlife), to sprout vegetation and to flood the River Nile.

The deceased kings embodied Osiris, and their children, the living Kings, embodied Horus (the son of Osiris).

Seth

Seth (also known as **Setekh, Setesh,** or **Set**) was the god of storms, evil, desert, war and disorder. He was the son of Geb and Nut and his triad of consorts included his sister Nephthys and the foreign goddesses Astarte and Anat.

Seth was the envious sibling of Osiris who he killed to become the King of Egypt. He is represented as a canine body with square-tipped ears, forked tail and a curved, long, projecting stout.

Ra

God of the sun and radiance, Ra (Re or Pra) was a solar deity whose reign extended far and wide. He was the ruler of the earth, sun and the underworld. Ra is linked with the hawk and falcon; the sun disc was his symbol. He was the second most powerful deity but was often wary of other gods supplanting him. His paranoia went to the extent of forbidding Nut from giving birth to deities that he feared would overthrow him; however, his scheme ended up being a tenuous one and Nut gave birth to major gods and goddesses, among whom was Isis, his wife and his fiercest rivalry.

Another rivalry was Apep (or Apophis), the god of chaos.He was Ra's arch-nemesis.He dwelled just below the horizon line and would swallow Ra every time he made his way to the underworld. When he would swallow Ra the sun would set and when he would completely devour him, night would come. Fortunately, he would fall by the wayside as he would always spit out Ra. This leads to sun rise.

His consorts were Hathor, Isis, and, in accordance with some accounts, Sekhmet and Bast.

According to certain cult-followers, Ra is viewed as the god who created the world and whose tears created men. He is also accredited for the formation of deities who were also his offspring—most were experiments of vengeance and protection against humanity. Sekhmet was the "eye of Ra"; Bast, the "cat of Ra"; and Hathor, the "eye of Ra."

Many gods merged with Ra, among them were Atum (Atum-Ra or Ra-Atum) andAmun(Amun-Ra).

Nephthys

Nephthys was a goddess that ruled over the night, rivers, death, water, service, protection and mourning. Like her twin sister Isis she was linked to funerary rites. This was because of the role her and her sister had in protecting the mummies and Osiris. She was depicted as either a kite or a woman with outstretched falcon wings, signifying protection.

Nephthys was the wife of Seth but her child Anubis is a mysterious subject. According to a myth, she was forbidden a child by Seth, so she contrived a plan in which she disguised herself as her sister Isis and seduced him. From this seduction was born Anubis. In fear of

Seth learning of this mischief and later being driven to kill the child, Nephthys pleaded with Isis to adopt Anubis as her own son. This explains why, as the adopted son of Osiris, Anubis became the underworld's ruler but was never able to take Osiris' position as he wasn't his real son.

Nut

The sister and consort of Geb, Nut was the mother of the major deities Nephthys, Isis, Osiris, and Seth. Her reign spanned over many realms; Nut was the Goddess of the sky, stars, the sun, light, the moon,astronomy, heaven, the universe, winds, and the air.

Nut personified the sun and the earth and was portrayed as either a nude women above the earth covered with stars or a cow.

Nut participated in saving Osiris and was thus seen as a friend of the dead. Upon his death Osiris pleaded:

"O my Mother Nut, stretch Yourself over me, that I may be placed among the imperishable stars which are in You, and that I may not die."

Nut was believed to welcome the deceased into her starry sky and nurture them:

"I am Nut, and I have come so that I may enfold and protect you from all things evil."

Anubis

Anubis (or Anpu) was the ruler of death, the underworld and funerals. He mummified the corpse of the dead and protected tombs. Anubis was the child of Seth and Nephthys — who was never told of the secret of his fatherhood. Anubis was also the adopted child of Isis and Osiris.

There are sources that posit Ra and Hesat or Bast as the parents of Anubis. Plutarch (c. 40–120 AD) states that Anubis is the illegitimate son of Osiris and Nephthys.

In the statue of Hermanubis it reads:

"For when Isis found out that Osiris loved her sister and had sexual relations with her in mistaking her sister for herself, and when she saw a proof of it in the form of a garland of clover that he had left to Nephthys - she was looking for a baby, because Nephthys abandoned it at once after it had been born for fear of Seth; and when Isis found the baby helped by the dogs which with great difficulties lead her there, she raised him and he became her guard and ally by the name of Anubis."

A jackal or a man with a head of a jackal was often the illustration of Anubis. His attributes included a flail, often held in his arm's crook, and a fetish.

His art of embalming was first practiced on the body of Osiris; he is accredited with the creation of the craft.

Bast

Bast (**Bastet, Baast, Ubaste,** or**Baset**) was the cat-headed goddess of love,protection, cats, warfare, music, joy and dance. She was the child of Isis and Ra.

Before the union of the two cultures of Egypt, Bast was Lower Egypt's warfare-goddess. Her counterpart in the opposite side Egypt was Sekhmet who was the warrior lioness deity of Upper Egypt. Although many deities merged after the union of Lower and Upper Egypt, these goddesses didn't follow suit. Bast transformed from a warrior lioness to a guardian deity during the Twenty-Second Dynasty (c. 945–715 BC).

In the 1st millennium BC, Bast was depicted as a cat-faced woman. In her later depictions in the eleventh century BCE, she was portrayed as either a lioness or a cat-headed woman carrying sistrum (sacred rattle) and an aegis.

Bast was not only the daughter of Ra but also his experimental instrument of vengeance. She was the one who beheaded the god of chaos Apophis who was the arch-nemesis of Ra. Bast was styled the "eye of Ra." According to a Myth, Ra sends her to the land of Nubia in disguise of a lioness.

Sekhmet

Sekhmet (or **Sachmis**) was the goddess of war, vengeance, medicine and fire. Her attributes were a sun disk, lioness and red linen. She was represented as either a large cat or a lioness; as a solar deity, she wore a solar disc and a Uraeus (a sacred serpent) which linked her to royalty and Wadjet.

To Egyptians she was the fiercest hunter whose breath instantaneously transformed land into a desert. She protected the pharaohs and spearheaded their wars.

She carried similar traits to the goddess Bast. They both had similar roles in Lower and Upper Egypt and both were the children and instruments of Ra. Sekhmet was "the eye of Ra", who was the fiercest weapon against the perils of humanity.

According to one myth, she was sent to finish the job Ra had sent Hathor to carry out—the eradication of the human race. Once she arrived, Sekhmet accidentally drunk beer thinking it was blood and ends up being too drunk to finish off the job of slaying humanity.

Amun

Amun was the god of the wind and the King of the deities (or Father of the deities). He and his wife Amaunet have been mentioned since the old Kingdom.

From the 11th to 16th century BC he rose to chief importance after his merge with the sun god Ra. He came to be known as Amun-Ra or Amen-Ra. The chief of all deities, Amun-Ra was the patron of the poor, the troubled and was the epicenter of personal piety.

Those who sought the help of Amun-Ra had to first confess their sins. The temple of Deir el-Medina reads:

"[Amun] who comes at the voice of the poor in distress, who gives breath to him who is wretched. You are Amun, the Lord of the silent, who comes at the voice of the poor; when I call to you in my distress. You come and rescue me...Though the servant was disposed to do evil, the Lord is disposed to forgive. The Lord of Thebes spends not a whole day in anger; His wrath passes in a moment; none remains. His breath comes back to us in mercy. May your ka be kind; may you forgive; It shall not happen again."

Maat

Maat was the goddess of truth and justice. Her attributes were a feather and an ostrich. Maat was the daughter of Ra and according to some sources the consort of Thoth.

Her role in the creation and her indefatigable struggle to preclude the universe from collapsing into chaos was significant. In her later function she handled the "weighing of the heart" (also called the "weighing of the souls"). This was carried out at Duat, in the underworld. Her feather was the determiner of whether the souls of the dead would successfully reach the utopia of the next world.

Often viewed as a female deity, Maat was in truth seen as the personification of the general principles of truth, justice, harmony, balance, morality and order; these were the ethics that every Egyptian had to follow. They were to act honorably and sincerely when dealing with matters of the community, family, god, the environment and their country.

CHAPTER III

Pharaohs of Ancient Egypt

The Pharaoh in Egypt during the ancient times was the ruler of the people. They were given the titles "High Priest of Every Temple" and "Lord of the Two Lands".

The first dynasties emerged in Egypt in 3000 BCE with the amalgamation of the Lower and Upper Egypt. These Pharaohs were considered gods on earth. After their demise, it was widely believed that they were to become the god of dead, Osiris. It was also the duty of the pharaohs to establish great monuments and temples in giving respect to the deities and in celebration of their success.

Tutankhamun

Tutankhamun (also called "King Tut" and Tutankhamen) is amongst the famous Egyptian Pharaoh of the eighteenth dynasty during the era of Egyptian history known as New Kingdom. The meaning of his name is "living image of [the god] Amun". Tutankhamun is a widely recognized pharaoh today—much like a celebrity— when Howard Carter, an archaeologist, unearthed his tomb (in 1922 CE) which was almost intact in the Valley of the Kings. Though Tutankhamun was considered an insubordinate leader, whose time of rule had hardly any influence, there was an about-face as more evidence started to emerge. At present, Tutankhamun is deemed to be an imperative figure that restored peace and order in a land where chaos was rife, and if it wasn't for his untimely death, he would have unequivocally contributed a great deal to Egypt's history.

Early Life

Amenhotep IV (also called Akhenaten) was the father of Tutankhamun. Amenhotep's wife was Nefertiti (the step-mother of Tutankhamun). Tutankhamun's mother was Lady Kiya. She was one of the lesser wives of Amenhotep. Lady Kiya was not Nefertiti (although a common mistaken view). According to some suggestions, Amenhotep III and Tiye, his queen, were the parents of Tutankhamun, nevertheless this theory is refuted by most scholars.

Ankhesenpaaten, Akhenaten and Nefertiti's fourth daughter, was engaged to Tutankhamun during his childhood years. Ankhesenpaaten was Tutankhamun's half-sister. Ankhesenpaaten was also thought to be older than he was, as she was wedded to her father previously (which she had a daughter from). Historian Margaret Bunson argues that at the time when Tutankhamun ascended to the throne at the age of eight, Ankhesenpaaten was thirteen-years old. Tutankhamun's early life entailed the death of his mother. He had to then live with his step-mother, father, and half-siblings in the palace at Amarna.

Small royalty symbols (for instance the flail and crook) were found in Tutankhamun's tomb. It is probable that, during his childhood, he played with them— in preparation for future rule.

According to Egyptologist ZahiHawass:

"A number of these [items] were inscribed with his birth name, demonstrating that he was crowned as Tutankhaten"

Reign

Following the death of his father, Tutankhamun ascended to the throne when he was just eight or nine-years old in 1338 or 1336 BC. Given his age, it was most probable that Tutankhamun was surrounded with very influential had advisors, most likely including the Vizier Ay and General Horemheb.

There was a temporary Pharaoh called Smenkhkare between Amenhotep's death and Tutankhamun's ascension to the throne. Very little is known about this Pharaoh. As Smenkhkare's throne name matched that of Akhenaten's coregent, it was thought that Nefertiti was this pharaoh who reigned during the time Akhenaten's wellbeing may have been deteriorating and Tutankhamun was incapable of taking the position of a leader because he was still too young.

During his reign 1332–1323 BC, Tutankhamun restored balanced and made several changes to the chaos Akhenaten put the nation into. Hawass writes:

"By the reign of Tutankhamun the situation in the *Near East* had changed drastically since the golden days of the Egyptian empire."

His restoration included establishing projects, particularly at Thebes and Karnak, where a temple was dedicated to Amun. Several monuments were built. The historian Barbra Watterson writes:

"He was said to be a king who spent his life making images of the gods, and it was during his reign that work on the colonnade in Luxor Temple with its superb scenes of the Opet Festival, was undertaken".

Tutankhamun, at just 16-years old, had to shoulder a great deal of onus of mending the nation his father had devastated all alone. The young king, even with the assistance of the senior advisors who encircled him, learned his situation overwhelming; he, nevertheless, strived to redeem his nation's present condition from its past. Unfortunately, his abbreviated life (died before reaching 20) was unable to show us what he might have accomplished in later years.

Tutankhamun's Death

Tutankhamun's death has remained the subject of considerable debate for centuries. There have been major studies carried out to figure out the grounds to his death. Early historians claim that he was murdered based on the damage of his skull. There are also speculations that Tutankhamun death was due to untreated tooth which was abscessed or from a fractured leg which had become infected. These theories, nevertheless, have been also refuted. According to another theory, Tutankhamun was not prone to a long life as he was as he was the outcome of incestuous union. Apologists of this theory cite Tutankhamun and Ankhesenamun's two stillborn children as physical proof of the practices of incest by the 18th dynasty Egyptian pharaohs. The only thing that is known is that the recorded date of the death of Tutankhamun was in January 1327 BC and that his life was cut short by an accident.

Cleopatra VII

Cleopatra VII Philopator, simply called Cleopatra, was born in 69 BCE and ruled together with Ptolemy XII Auletes, her father. At the age of eighteen, she ascended to the throne after her father died. Since it was mandatory in the Egyptian tradition that a male consort was needed for a woman to rule, Ptolemy XIII, her 12-year old brother, was wedded to her. But soon after, she dropped the name of her brother from all documents that were official and reigned alone. Cleopatra (unlike the other Ptolemy rulers who reigned for centuries in Egypt without knowing the language) had a great command over the Egyptian language and was articulate in Greek (her native language). She was also skilled in other languages. She therefore needed no help from translators to communicate with diplomats from other nations.

Historian Plutarch writes:

"it was a pleasure merely to hear the sound of her voice, with which, like an instrument of many strings, she could pass from one language to another; so that there were few of the barbarian nations that she answered by an interpreter."

Her prompt action in regards to decision making without her counselors created disgruntlement amongst some of the prominent officials. Pothinus, her head advisor, General Achillas, and Theodotus of Chios in 48 BCE dethroned her and made Ptolemy XIII the ruler, assuming he would be much controllable than Cleopatra. Cleopatra and Arsinoe (her half-sister) fled to Thebaid.

Pompey, Ptolemy and Caesar

Around the same period, Pompey the Great, the Roman politician and general, was overpowered at the Battle of Pharsalus by Julius

Caesar in the autumn of 48 BC. In seek of sanctuary, Pompey fled to Alexandria to get away from the forces of Caesar, however, what awaited him was much different. He was beheaded under the gaze of the young Ptolemy XIII— only thirteen-years old at that time— and his children and wife from the ship which he had just got off from. It is said to be that Ptolemy, who ordered Pompey's death, did it to curry favor with Caesar, therefore becoming Rome's ally, to which, at that moment, Egypt was indebted to.

Upon his arrival in Egypt with his legions 2 days later, however, Caesar was infuriated when the head of Pompey was presented to him by Ptolemy. Even though Pompey was the political foe of Caesar, he was a consul of Rome and the widower of Julia, the only rightful daughter of Caesar who died during childbirth. Caesar announced government by the army and established himself in the palace of the royals. Ptolemy XIII, with his court, escaped to Pelusium; however, Caesar was not going to permit the young leader to slip away and stir trouble so he had him return back to Alexandria.

Caesar & Cleopatra's Relationship

For Cleopatra, this was the time to make use of the fury of Julius Caesar toward Ptolemy. Still in exile, Cleopatra knew the possibility of entering the palace without being pestered was slim. She therefore had herself covertly smuggled into the royal palace. This endeavor was made successful as she was rolled in a rug (supposedly a present for the general of Rome) to meet Caesar. They both seemed to develop instant attraction for each other. Caesar and Cleopatra were already in a relationship by the time Ptolemy XIII came to see Caesar the following morning. Ptolemy was fuming.

Nine month later, Cleopatra, in June of 47 BCE, gave birth to Ptolemy Caesar (also called Caesarion, meaning "little Caesar") and stated him publicly her successor.

Caesar deserted his objective to annex Egypt. To the contrary, he defended the claim of Cleopatra to the throne. The forces of Ptolemy was overpowered by Caesar at the Battle of the Nile, and in an attempt to escape after the battle, Ptolemy drowned in the Nile. The other leaders who were apart of the group in opposition to Cleopatra were also killed during the battle or afterwards.

Rome saw the return of Caesar in 46 BCE. Soon after his return, Caesar brought Cleopatra and their son, together with her whole staff to reside there. He acknowledged publicly that Caesarion was his offspring, but not as his heir, as he chose Octavian, his grandnephew, instead. He also acknowledged Cleopatra as being his spouse, albeit he had a wife named Calpurnia Pisons at that time. This situation caused rage amongst the several senates and the public for the rules of Rome against bigamy were firmly stuck to.

The assassination of Caesar took place on the 15th of March, 44 BC, while Cleopatra was still in Rome with her entire staff.

Mark Antony & Cleopatra

Following the assassination of Caesar, Cleopatra fled the country with her son and entourage to Alexandria. Mark Antony, the right-hand man of Caesar, together Lepidus and Octavian were in pursuit of defeating the conspirators that were responsible for murdering Caesar. Following the Battle of Philipi, at which the armed forces of Octavian and Antony triumphed, Antony became the ruler of the provinces in the east, including Egypt, while the west was ruled by Octavian.

Cleopatra, in 41 BC, was summoned by Antony in Tarsus to give answers about her faithfulness. During the Roman war, allegedly, she paid considerable amount of cash to Cassius and Brutus. Cleopatra's flamboyant arrival charmed Antony.

Plutarch writes:

"She came sailing up the river Cydnus in a barge with gilded stern and outspread

sails of purple, while oars of silver beat time to the music of flutes and fifes and harps. She herself lay all along, under a canopy of cloth of gold, dressed as Venus in a picture, and beautiful young boys, like painted Cupids, stood on each side to fan her. Her maids were dressed like Sea Nymphs and Graces, some steering at the rudder, some working at the ropes...perfumes diffused themselves from the vessel to the shore, which was covered with multitudes, part following the galley up the river on either bank, part running out of the City to see the sight. The market place was quite emptied, and Antony at last was left alone sitting upon the tribunal while the word went, through all the multitude, that Venus was come to feast with Bacchus for the common good of Asia."

Cleopatra and Mark Antony became lovers right away and lasted together for ten years. Their offspring's were three. Cleopatra was also considered by Antony as his wife, although he was first wedded to Fulvia and then to Octavian's sister, Octavia. He divorced Octavia eventually to be wedded to Cleopatra legally.

Cleopatra's Death

Octavian and Antony's ailing relationship crumbled during these years that even a civil war was engendered. Both the armies of Cleopatra and Antony were overpowered, in 31 BC, by the armed forces of Octavian at the Battle of Actium. They both ended their lives a year later. Antony, upon falsely hearing that Cleopatra died, stabbed himself with his sword and came to find out that she was alive after it was too late. Octavian permitted Antony to be taken to Cleopatra. It was in her arms that he died. The situation for Cleopatra was unfavorable and she understood that she would be taken to Rome as captive, mainly to embellish the victory of Octavian. Cleopatra knew there was no possible way that Octavian would be manipulated like Antony and Caesar, so, she asked for some time to get ready. She was allowed the time that she demanded. It was then that Cleopatra managed to make a snake (conventionally an asp, although it is thought to be an Egyptian cobra by a large amount of scholars nowadays) bite her to be poisoned.

Cleopatra's son Caesarion was slaughtered after being captured by the orders of Octavian and her three children by Antony were raised by Octavia in Rome. This ended the lineage of the pharaohs in Egypt.

Ramses II

Ramses II (also known as: Ramesses II, Rameses, Ramses the Great and known as *Userma'atre'setepenre* by the Egyptian, meaning *"Keeper of Harmony and Balance, Strong in Right, Elect of Ra"*, also called Ozymandias) was one of the Pharaohs (the third) of the nineteenth Dynasty. Ramesses lived till the age of 96. His concubines and wives in total exceeded two-hundred and had over 150 children. He outlived most of his children.

Early Life

The parents of Ramesses were Queen Tuya and Seti I. When he was 14-years old, he attended military campaigns with his father, including Palestine and Libya. Ramses was spearheading the campaigns he made himself in Nubia at the age of 22 with his two sons. He was named the co-ruler with Seti.

Ramses, with his father, planned big projects which included restorations and established a palace at Avaris. Ramses ascended to power following the death of his father in 1290 BC and without further ado commenced military operation in an effort to reinstate Egypt's borders and to guarantee trade routes.

Literally hundreds of buildings, temples and monuments were built by Ramesses, including the two rock temples at Abu Simbel. It is considered by several historians that his reign is the peak of Egyptian art and culture.

Queen Nefertari

Ramesses' first wife and favorite queen was Nefertari. During the rule of Ramesses several depictions of her appeared in statuary and temple walls. This was despite her rather early death (possibly during child birth).

Ramses married Istnofret after Nefertari's death. And following the death of Istnofret, his daughters became his consorts. Be that as it may, he couldn't simply forget about his beloved wife Nefertari. He had her portrait carved on statuary and walls long after marrying other women.

Thutmose III

Thutmose III (also known as Tuthmosis III, Thothemes or Thutmosis) was the 6th king of the 18th Dynasty. He is often called "The Napoleon of Ancient Egypt." Thutmose is often regarded as the best pharaoh ancient Egypt has ever seen. He was a national hero responsible for the golden age of ancient Egypt. Thutmose III ruled from 1479 BC to 1425 BC.

Early Life

Thutmose III was the son of Thutmose II; his mother, Iset, was one of his father's secondary wives. Given that there was no prince with a better claim to the throne, Thutmose was crowned king on the early death of his father in 1479 BC. He was, however, very young (only seven years-old) to rule at that time, so Hatshepsut (his father's chief wife) ruled on her own while Thutmose III was gaining military training most of the time.

Thutmose III had several wives which he had nine children from.

Military Campaigns

Amongst Thutmose III's greatest achievement as a Pharaoh of Egypt were his military campaigns. He by and large initiated at least 16 military campaigns including those in Syria, Palestine, Nubia and Mesopotamia.

According to historians, Thutmose III disliked his aunt and co-regent Hatshepsut. She was not a warrior and permitted neighbors of Egypt to believe they could liberate themselves from Egypt. His former years spent in the army made him an ingenious warrior who was valiant and not afraid to engage in battles. During his reign, he conquered approximately 350 cities and obtained complete respect of Egypt and the entire region. In order to keep conquered leaders from raiding Egypt, Thutmose III required that they send their children to Egypt for their education. This very much deterred potential attacks.

Thutmose III's Tomb

It was in the Valley of the Kings (one of the most sophisticated tombs) that Thutmose III was buried. Inside the tomb, only the wooden statues of the king and other gods, the red quartzite sarcophagus, pottery, bits of wooden model boats and the bones of animals were found. Even Thutmose III's mummy wasn't inside the tomb upon its discovery. He was buried at Deir el-Bahri, the mortuary temple of Hatshepsut. The condition of Thutmose III's mummy was bad when it was found. The ruler was short, not even five feet tall.

Akhenaten

Akhenaten (also called 'Ikhnaton', 'Khuenaten' or 'Akhenaton'— they all mean "successful for" or "of great use to" the god Aten) was a pharaoh of the Eighteen Dynasty. After converting to the cult of Aten, he changed his name from Amenhotep IV (or Amenophis IV) to Akhenaten. It was during his reign that the empire began to crumble.

The youngest son of the Chief Queen Tiye and Amenhotep III, he was the consort of Queen Nefertiti and the father of Tutankhamun (by Lady Kiya) and Tutankhamen's wife Ankhesenamun(by Nefertiti). As Amenhotep IV, his reign lasted for five years in which he respected the venerated traditions of the Egyptian religion and adhered to his father's policies. However, in the fifth year of his reign, he made dramatic religious transformations. It began with his change of religion from the cult of Amun to that of Aten. For the following decade he pursued a campaign of establishing the superior religion of Aten in Egypt (becoming the first king to institute monotheism) and emaciated Egypt's tradition of polytheism. He came to be infamously known as the 'Heretic king'.

Foreign Policy

One unfortunate result of Akhenaten's religious reforms was the neglect of foreign policy. According to the sources, other countries, former associates of Egypt, wrote several times in seek of Egypt's assistance but were elbowed aside by Akhenaten. The king simply made the choice to ignore what happens outside Egypt's borders. He also gave little notice to affairs outside his palace at Akhetaten.

CHAPTER IV

Book of the Dead: Life, Death and Afterlife

There were a lot of beliefs in ancient Egypt and most of them revolved around life, death and the afterlife. And thanks to the historians and archeologists, who have shed their blood and sweat to unravel these mysteries, we are now able to understand the mindset and viewpoints of ancient Egyptians.

Book of the Dead

Book of the Dead is, without a doubt, one of ancient Egypt's greatest relics. It was one of the earliest literary works to elaborately illustrate the nation's funerary traditions; the concept of life, death and the afterlife. But the practice of funerary writing in Egypt dates back to the Old Kingdom, the 24th century B.C.

The first kinds of obituary writing in Egypt were Pyramid Texts, which were inscribed on the walls of burial chamber in pyramids. Pyramid texts, which included several figures representing humans and animals, were purposed to protect and help dead kings pass on to the afterlife safely. And the first of this kind of writing was used in the pyramid of King Unas, during the 24th century B.C.

Then during the reign of the Middle Kingdom, Pyramid texts evolved to what is called Coffin Texts. The contents of the Coffin Text had much similarity to that of the Pyramid Text. But there certainly were obvious discrepancies; one was that this new form of funerary text was inscribed on the interiors of a coffin, sometimes on Papyri or the walls of a tomb but mostly on the surface of coffins; secondly, unlike the Pyramid Texts, which were used only by the royals and the elite; the Coffin Text was available for the commoners as well.

Then with the rise of the New kingdom which was around 1550 B.C. Egyptian writing and funerary tradition underwent yet another telling evolution, which was marked by the surfacing of the 'Book of the Dead'.

The *Book of the Dead* which is read as **'Reu nu pert emhru'** in Egyptian, and means '*The Chapters of coming forth by day*' or '*Book of emerging forth into the Light*' is an entity that highlighted the period of the New Kingdom. It was during this time that it developed and gained widespread recognition. Historians say that it existed until the 1st century B.C.

The *Book of the Dead* is a funerary scripture aimed at facilitating an easy and safe navigation through the Duat (the underworld) for the dead. It was also believed that this entity would enable the deceased to get help and protection from the Gods during this challenging journey.

It is basically a collection of spells, some were new but most of them were collected from the Pyramid Texts and Coffin Texts. It was written on a papyrus commissioned by the individual before death or by a relative. The quality of the papyri and the texts differed tremendously, and it all depended upon the individual's financial stand.

Papyri were very expensive during that period and only the royals or the elite were able to afford them. There was even a point where archeologists discovered a *Book of the Dead* written on a second-hand papyrus.

The *Book of the Dead*, at certain occasions, would be written on linen shrouds, which would be used to wrap the dead bodies.

As earlier stated, the *Book of the Dead* is a compilation of magical spells written over the course of about one thousand years. The spells were written in the form of cursive hieroglyphs which were arranged in columns and separated by a black line. Each text, inscribed by a black or red ink, is accompanied by a certain kind of illustration.

There was a great amount of variety in the type of vignettes utilized in the *Book of the Dead*; some were extravagant, colorful, rich and large, whereas others were very simple and small, as in line drawings.

Often times, the illustrations included the image of the deceased's wife; but drawing of vicious lions, crocodiles, snakes, beetles and hippopotamus were also quite common.

Each *Book of the Dead* was unique and different. There was no order or pattern in the way the chapters of the *Book of the Dead* were arranged. The illustrations, the texts, the spells were all developed in a way that's to satisfy the preference of the deceased or their relatives.

So far about 192 spells used in ancient Egypt and in the *Book of the Dead* are known. But there isn't a single *Book of the Dead* that contains all these spells, and if there is, well, it hasn't yet been found then.

The greatest and most explicit relic of this funerary tradition that has survived for this long and still is in a good condition is The Papyrus of Ani – a legacy of ancient Egypt and one that is currently situated in The British Museum, London.

Here are some of the translated spells historians and archeologists have managed to unravel.

"O you Soul [ba], greatly majestic, behold, I have come that I may see you; I open the Netherworld that I may see my father Osiris and drive away darkness, for I am beloved of him. I have come that I may see my father Osiris and that I may cut out the heart of Seth who has harmed my father Osiris. I have opened up every path which isin the sky and on earth, for I am the well-beloved son of my father Osiris. I am noble, I am a spirit [akh], I am equipped; O all you gods and all you spirits [akhu], prepare a path for me."

— Spell 9 from the Papyrus of Ani

"All the evil which was on me has been removed.

What does that mean? It means that I was cleansed on the day of my birth in the two great and noble marshes which are in Heracleopolis on the day when the common folk make offerings to the Great God who is therein.
What are they? 'Eternity' is the name of one; 'sea' is the name of the other. They are the Lake of Natron and the Lake of Maat.
Otherwise said: 'Eternity governs' is the name of one; 'Sea' is the name of the other.'
Otherwise said: 'Seed of Eternity' is the name of one; 'sea' is the name of the other. As for that Great God who is therein, he is Ra himself'"

—— **Spell 17, from the Papyrus of Ani.**

If challenged by questions in the afterlife, this was used to demonstrate one's acquaintance with religion and its secrets.

"I have put my name in the Upper Egyptian shrine, I [have] made my name to be remembered in the Lower Egyptian shrine, on this night of counting the years and of numbering the months."

—Spell 25, from Book of the Dead.

It was used to help the deceased remember their names after death.

Life

No amount of fame or fortune can equate the worth of life; it is a priceless entity that could never be sold or exchanged. But life for ancient Egyptians was just a segment, a very small part of the eternal journey that awaited them after death.

Bunson, the historian, argues that ancient Egyptians believed that human life, its goal and purpose, was to simply serve as a phase of life through which one could acquire eternal happiness offered in life after death.

But to accomplish a harmonious eternal journey one must live a good and just life here on earth.

Death

Death in Egyptian mythology doesn't quite necessarily mean the end. It is viewed as the moment when the soul parts from the body and is brought before Osiris in the "Hall of Truth" for the final judgment. The god Anubis is said to be the one who escorts the soul to Osiris.

However, before the soul stands to face Osiris and the final judgment, he/she must first pass through a series of gates and caverns that are infiltrated and guarded by mystical creatures that are vicious and will do whatever is possible to stop the passer-by. And to pacify these ferocious beings the deceased would use the spells in his/her *Book of the Dead.*

"Get back! Retreat! Get back, you dangerous one! Do not come against me, do not live by my magic; may I not have to tell this name of yours to the Great God who sent you; 'Messenger' is the name of one, and Bedty is the name of the other. The crocodile speaks: 'Your face belongs to righteousness. The sky encloses the stars, magic encloses its settlements, and my mouth encloses themagic which is in it. My teeth are a knife, my tusks are the Viper Mountain. The deceased replied: 'O you with a spine who would work your mouth against this magic of mine, no crocodile which lives by magic shall take it away"

—Spell 31, used to stop the attack of crocodiles.

And if the deceased manages to circumvent all the obstacles and passes through all the challenges, then he/she will be escorted to the Hall of Truth.

In the Hall of Truth, the deceased would then be asked to swear that he/she did not commit the 42 sins, which are also known as the "Negative Confession".

Here are some of the sins on the list:

I have not committed sin.

I have not committed robbery with violence.

I have not stolen.

I have not slain men and women.

I have not stolen grain.

I have not purloined offerings.

I have not stolen the property of the gods.

I have not uttered lies.

I have not carried away food.

I have not uttered curses.

I have not committed adultery.

I have made none to weep.

After reciting the Negative Confession before the 42 judges, the heart, which is seen as the base of intelligence and memory, would then be put on a golden scale against the white feather of Maat or Ma'at and get weighed.

The deceased would be considered as someone who has lived a life free of sins and will be granted entrance to the afterlife, if the heart weighs lighter than the feather. But if the heart weighs heavier than the feather, then the soul of the deceased would be thrown to the underworld where the merciless monster Ammut would devour it.

To avoid such calamity, ancient Egyptians would always take measures to protect and give the much needed strength to the deceased's heart. There were two common ways they would execute this ritual and one was done through magical spells like the kind depicted in Spell 125 or Spell 30B which reads,

"O my heart of my mother! O my heart of my mother! O my heart of my different forms! Do not stand up as a witness against me, do not be opposed to me in the tribunal, do not be hostile to me in the presence of the Keeper of the Balance, for you are my ka which was in my body, the protectorwho made my members hale. Go forth to the happy place where to we speed, do not make my name stink to the Entourage who make men. Do not tell lies about me in the present of the god. It is indeed well that you should hear!"

— Spell 30B

The other method ancient Egyptians commonly used for the protection of the deceased's heart was the burying of the body with a heart shaped scarabs.

Afterlife

In Egyptian mythology the afterlife is a place of eternal bliss; the anxiously awaited paradise where only the gods and the pure would be able to live in. The illustration of the afterlife in Egyptian mythology is quite diverse, but most commonly it is imagined to be a rich and green place, where there were plenty waterways, crops, people, oxen and so forth.

The afterlife is often referred to as the 'Field of Reeds' in the *Book of the Dead*; it's represented as a place that has much similarity to that of life on earth.

In the afterlife it is believed that the deceased will be able to join the Great Ennead (a group of gods) and his or her parents. It was also stated in various scriptures that once the deceased passes the judgment and enters the afterlife, he/she will not only join Osiris and all the other supreme Gods but will also possess some kind of a divine power as well. This belief is illustrated by the way each *Book of the Dead* starts out as "The Osiris - [Name of the deceased]".

The *Book of the Dead* clearly depicts the marvelous aspects of the afterlife, but it also states that it was mandatory for the deceased to take part in a number of laborious chores. For this reason, the burial mounds would often have several statuettes with spells written on them; these objects were called Shabti or Ushebti.

CHAPTER V

Rituals and Sacrifices

As in many countries and cultures around the world in bygone days, Egypt also had rituals and believed in making sacrifices, human or otherwise.

Rituals

Ancient Egyptians preformed various kinds of rituals for various reasons; to maintain peace and order in the world, to protect the dead, to seek guidance, help and so forth. It's no different than how the modern day society goes to church, synagogues, mosques, or temples to pray, praise or give out offerings.

Daily offering ceremonies in temples were one of the most commonly practiced rituals in ancient Egypt. Offering food, clothing, carvings, weapons, tools and so forth was a way of honoring and caring for the gods that have created them. These daily ritual were supervised by temple priests.

Private rituals, such as hymning or evoking mythical events, were also preformed, but these were often referred to as 'magical' and they were for the purpose of healing an illness or getting protection.

Breaking red pots after it's been used for purification by water was also a customary ritual. It was part of the funerary tradition, which was purposed to protect the dead from their enemies or evil spirits.

These pots had inscriptions of the enemy's name and breaking it symbolized their destruction.

"3 times half loaf offerings and reversion of offerings, 3 times removing the footprints and breaking of the red pots, once lay (down) the royal offering, wash, sit down by the offering, once libation water, incense fire, an offering which the king gives to the Osiris Ni-ankh-pepi"

— Rule of this ritual from the Unas- cemetery, Mastaba of Ni-anch-Pepi

Sacrifices

Blood sacrifice was regarded as the most supreme form of rituals in ancient Egypt. It seen as a very powerful way of appeasing the gods.

Initially, animals were the only creatures that were sacrificed. Bulls, for instance, were symbolized as the god Taurus, who had features of both human and animal. So sacrificing the bull was seen as a way of giving the gods a noble gift – a demigod.

Crocodiles were also commonly slaughtered, as they symbolized Seth at Edfu and Dendera.

Then with the course of time, Egyptians began to sacrifice humans. During human sacrificial ceremonies, the victims would first be treated and honored as gods before the killing. Historians believe that most of the sacrificial victims were criminals, rebels or prisoners of war.

According to the legends, criminals were sacrificed to appease the most powerful goddess in Egyptian mythology, Sekhmet, who was killed by a rebellious person.

BONUS CHAPTER

Ten Little Known Facts about Egyptian Mythology

Egyptians kept animals as pets

Animals in ancient Egypt were greatly valued. They were treated with respect and profound affection.

So many different kinds of animals were raised as cherished pets in almost every household in Egypt. Cats and dogs were the most domesticated, but people also raised hoopoes, falcons, vervet monkeys, doves, geese, even lions and Sudanese cheetahs.

Ancient Egyptians loved their pets; as evidence shows they mourned at their death and did whatever was possible to heal their illness.

Ancient Egyptians loved Board Games

With the lapse of centuries a lot of things change. But the one thing that has never experienced even a slight wobble is how we entertain ourselves by way of playing games. It's a long lived human tradition that even ancient Egyptians can attest to.

Egyptians loved playing board games. After a long day of work they would gather and play the 'Mehen', 'Dogs and Jackals' or 'Senet' for hours. Even for the Pharaohs, board games were indispensable; Tutankhamen, for instance, was buried with several board games, and as several paintings show Queen Nefertari was also fond of playing Senet.

Pharaohs were often overweight

So many paintings illustrate the Pharaohs as slim and fit beings. But the truth about their figure is quite different.

There was no end or limit to the daily offerings in ancient Egypt. And one of the most commonly offered items was food. The majority of the society was vegetarian but for the pharaohs the people brought meals such as beef, bread, fruit, honey, cake, wine and beer, which were certainly luxurious but decadent. And as the remains of their bodies show, they certainly ate well and gained quite a lot of excess fat.

Studies show that most of them were diabetic and suffered from vascular calcification. The mummy of Queen Hatshepsut serves as the perfect example.

The Pyramids were not built by slaves

The Pyramid is one of ancient Egypt's greatest and most astonishing relics. What inspired its formation is one aspect that could pique anyone's interest, but what's more amazing is how it wasn't constructed by slaves.

This majestic entity was actually built by skilled construction workers who weren't exploited but paid for their services.

Most of Ancient Egypt Remains Uncovered

As the world's most historic destination, Egypt has attracted the attention of historians and archeologists who have certainly dedicated their time, knowledge and sweat to unravel her mysterious and colorful past. But it's a huge country with a huge amount of desert sand.

Recently, archaeologists have found evidence that could lead them to yet another pyramid. And this one is believed to be 4,300 years old and harbors the remains of the mother of pharaohs. So it's strongly believed that the world has yet to see more of ancient Egypt.

Women in Ancient Egypt

In ancient Egypt women were treated equally as men. In Egyptian mythology, goddesses were creators and protectors of the pharaohs; Ma'at, the goddess of balance and order; Nekhbet, the vulture goddess of Upper Egypt; Wadjet, the cobra goddess of Lower Egypt were but a few.

And so in society, women had equal, if not more, prominence as men. They had the liberty to participate in the economic, political and judicial arenas. They had the right to work, to divorce or remarry.

Pepi II: The Fly King

According to legends Pepi II was the Old Kingdom's last pharaoh. He ruled for over 64 years after acceding to the throne at the tender age of six.

Pepi is often styled the "Fly King" and that was because he despised flies. And what's interesting is how he would have naked slaves smeared in honey around him so as to keep the flies away.

Men Wore Makeup

Appearance is always something to care about. And in every generation women are known to be more self-conscious than men, but in ancient Egypt the men also worked equally as hard as women did on their appearance— yes, they wore makeup.

But they didn't quite necessarily wear make up for vanity, it was simply because they believed that it had magical healing powers. They would often apply this make up, which was called Kohl, around the eyes using a sort of a liner made out of wood, ivory and bone.

The First Labor Strike in History

Ancient Egyptians were strong people who stood up for what they believed in. They loved and respected their pharaohs, but they weren't afraid to fight back when their rights were being violated.

During the ruling days of the New Kingdom, in the 12th century B.C., there was a delay of payment for the laborers working at Deir el-Medina. The workers then, angered by this action, decided to organize a strike – the first in history. They entered a mortuary temple and demonstrated a sit-down until their demands were met. It wasn't long before they ended up getting their deserved pay.

The Death of Tutankhamen

The young pharaoh, Tutankhamen, lived a very short life. He died at a young age and there is very little account of the kind of life he lived before his passing. Regarding how he died, however, recent studies seem to have an answer.

Scan of his mummy shows that Tutankhamen was buried without his heart and chest wall, which meant that he died out of a terrible wound, as in the one caused by a vicious attack of a hippopotamus.

Legend has it that Egyptians loved hunting this creature and this young price was known for his love of hunting.

CPSIA information can be obtained
at www.ICGtesting.com
Printed in the USA
LVOW08s0030050517
533278LV00017B/1136/P